Sp[...]

Leo A. Menzweiler, a Master worker for the Morton F. Plant Hospital Foundation

With warm personal regards
Edward I. Imparato

INTO DARKNESS

INTO DARKNESS

A Pilot's Journey Through Headhunter Territory

By Edward T. Imparato

Designed by Carolyn Weary Brandt
Edited by Katherine A. Neale and Ross A. Howell, Jr.
© 1995 by Edward T. Imparato. All rights reserved.
This book, or any portions thereof, may not be reproduced or transmitted in any form or by any means, electronic or mechanical, including photocopying, recording, or by any information storage and retrieval system, without permission in writing from the copyright holder.

Manufactured in Hong Kong
Published by Howell Press, Inc., 1147 River Road, Suite 2, Charlottesville, Virginia 22901. Telephone (804) 977-4006.
First Printing

Library of Congress Cataloging-in-Publication Data

Imparato, Edward T.
    Into darkness: a pilot's journey through headhunter territory/
Edward T. Imparato.
    p. cm.
    Includes index.
    ISBN 0-943231-91-4

    1. World War, 1939-1945--Campaigns--New Guinea. 2. New Guinea--History. I. Title.

Acknowledgments

My sincere thanks to a number of individuals who made contributions to my work are in order: to Wendel Moseley, who first edited the manuscript; to Brian Burke, who wrote the synopsis for the benefit of the publisher; and to Marie DeMarko Schaub, who encouraged me to submit the manuscript to a publisher.

I owe a great debt of gratitude to my wife Jean, who read and reread the manuscript many times to assist me in making the manuscript as free of errors and omissions as possible, and to my typist, Janice DeMeza, whose patience and understanding were greatly appreciated.

I am especially indebted to Charles F. Hamilton, historian and author, for continued encouragement and counsel during the final stages of the assembly of the manuscript, the rewriting of certain passages for clarity, and the addition of new material concerning the details of the investigation at the crash site.

A very special thanks to Kate Neale, who was assigned to me by the publisher, Ross Howell, to edit the manuscript. Her skillful way with words and her fine-tuning of many sentences and paragraphs gave the manuscript a polish I could not have achieved alone.

Edward T. Imparato
Belleair, Florida

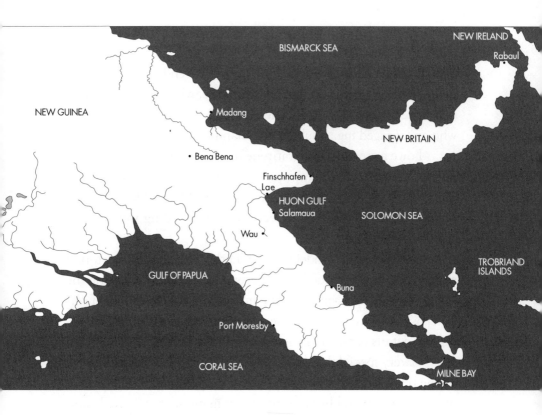

Contents

INTRODUCTION	i
CHAPTER I Briefing	1
CHAPTER II Port Moresby	19
CHAPTER III Air Raid	27
CHAPTER IV Preparations	34
CHAPTER V Outpost Bena Bena	40
CHAPTER VI Korefego	55
CHAPTER VII Uncontrolled Territory	75
CHAPTER VIII Tunofi Village	82
CHAPTER IX Sing-sing	89
CHAPTER X Burial	97
CHAPTER XI Amorika Village	103
CHAPTER XII Crash Site	108
CHAPTER XIII Debriefing	121
CHAPTER XIV New CO	128
EPILOGUE	132
TIMELINE	136
INDEX	138

Introduction

There's no good place to fight a war. There never was. There never will be. But as any soldier can tell you, some war zones are worse than others. There were many wretched places to fight during World War II: nobody had much good to say about the Aleutian Islands, for example, or the Sahara, or Russia in winter. But for those who served there, two of the worst spots in the war — maybe any war — lay far across the broad Pacific, a long way west of Waikiki. Burma was one; New Guinea was surely the other.

New Guinea and Burma shared a number of characteristics, all of them bad. Dreadful razorback ridges fell away into deep, vegetation-choked ravines where it was always twilight. Riotous tropical vegetation writhed and slithered everywhere, blotting out the daylight and eagerly eating up the tiny trails mere men had made. Where the country opened up a little, there were fetid swamps or forests of impenetrable kunai grass, which rasped men's skin like a file.

New Guinea and Burma seethed with armies of insects: mosquitoes, gnats, flies, leeches, and a hundred other crawling, flitting creatures made life ugly for soldiers on both sides. A dozen virulent diseases killed and crippled, and men suffered terribly from all manner of rot, itch, and fungus.

Sheets of rain added to the misery, suddenly turning little creeks into rushing, eager torrents. Trails became bogs of treacly mud that could suck the boots off a man's feet, and everything mildewed from the incessant heat and moisture. Soldiers' feet turned to puffy, shapeless blobs of fish-bellied flesh, rotten with trench foot and jungle fungus.

Into Darkness takes place in New Guinea in 1943, a brutal time in a brutal land. New Guinea is a huge island: shaped like a bird flying west towards Asia. The western part of New Guinea was under Dutch control before the war and the eastern half, including a piece of the north coast that had been a German colony prior to World War I, was administered by Australia. The southeastern part of the island — the long, trailing tailfeathers of the bird — was called Papua, and was, generally speaking, the most densely populated part of New Guinea.

Along the south coast of New Guinea, an area that time forgot, lay a very thin and very fragile veneer of civilization. This is where Port Moresby, New Guinea's major settlement, was located. There were cleared areas where people lived, towns and ports, even a road or two. But farther north, beyond the Coral Sea littoral, lay only darkness: brooding, aboriginal, abyssal darkness.

In Burma, on the other hand, the British — soldiers, policemen, administrators, and supervisors for the English timber companies — had pushed into nearly every corner of the country. To that extent, Burma was terra cognita, however tough and unforgiving the country was. And the British had friends among the hill tribes of Burma, tough little men who helped and guided British troops, and brought in Japanese ears in exchange for silver rupees.

New Guinea was different; it was 750,000 square miles of mystery. Once you got past the thin skin of the coast, the huge island was primeval darkness. Such order as there was, was kept by a handful of intrepid Aussie civil servants and policemen, backed by staunch Papuan "police boys" equipped with bolt action rifles.

But the King's Peace prevailed in the coastal areas along the major cross-island tracks. Farther inland, deep in the misty hills on both sides of the high, rugged Owen Stanley Range, lay thousands of square miles ominously labeled "uncontrolled" on the maps. Uncontrolled on a New Guinea map equated roughly with the legend "here be dragons," found in the empty spaces of old mariners' charts.

It was very bad country, this huge, uncontrolled emptiness. It was bad not only because of its riot of tropical vegetation and kunai grass, its swamps, and steep, tortuous hills, but also because of its swarms of insects and gooey mud and pervasive rot. And it was bad because of the people who lived there.

For people did live in the unpacified territory, a good many of them: suspicious, aboriginal people of fierce and belligerent disposition. They were cannibals, too, these wary, primitive folk. They ate their enemies, of course, but they also ate each other, even their own kin.

And so, when Ed Imparato and his scratch expedition pushed off into the great empty spaces where the map got vague, they walked into great danger. Other men had died in the interior, lots of them, including downed pilots. There was every chance that some of these fallen angels had also been eaten.

But the mission was worth it. For deep in that hostile wilderness north of Port Moresby might lie the answer to a life-and-death question: What was causing a series of noncombat crashes of the Consolidated B-24? The B-24 Liberator was a four-engine, all-purpose aircraft, a workhorse on which much of the Pacific air war depended. Combat casualties were bad enough, but these losses were intolerable: they apparently had nothing to do with the enemy or weather. Each crash cost the U.S. Army Air Force an invaluable airplane. Worse, each B-24 that disappeared carried ten highly trained young Americans to their deaths. Imparato's mission wouldn't make the history books, but it was critical to the successful prosecution of the air war.

Northeast of New Guinea, between the Bismarck and the Solomon Seas, lay the big island of New Britain, and at its most northeastern tip was the powerful Japanese base of Rabaul. Rabaul's marvelous natural anchorage could shelter any number of Japanese warships. The base's airstrips could support hundreds of aircraft, poised to hammer American men-of-war and merchant vessels. The island's storehouses were crammed with supplies, and its 100,000-man garrison was ready to fight to the death. A little further east of Rabaul lay Kavieng, on New Ireland, another concentration of Japanese strength.

Both strongholds would have to be captured or at least controlled before the transpacific advance could proceed. Allied forces had planned to capture Rabaul until July 1943, when Gen. George C. Marshall suggested to Gen. Douglas MacArthur that Rabaul need not be invaded at all. The great base could be battered prostrate and simply bypassed, said Marshall, an action that would require every available aircraft.

American and Australian aircraft might gradually win control of the air and sea. Once that critical control was won, America could bypass the great Japanese bases and push on toward the home islands of Japan.

Obviously, control of the air was all-important. Whoever held the air could hammer his enemy at will, protect his own troops from air attack, sink his enemy's ships, and strangle his enemy's bases. For this, the B-24 was a very useful weapon, a wonderfully versatile aircraft. More than eighteen thousand B-24s were produced during World War II, more than any other American military airplane.

The B-24 was flown by the Royal Air Force (RAF) and other British Commonwealth air forces, as well as by the U.S. Army Air Force (USAAF). It could do just about anything the Allies needed done. It had originally been designed as a heavy bomber, with a long range and a bombload of between four and four and one-half tons. On short runs, a maximum effort using exterior bomb racks, the big plane could haul as much as twelve thousand pounds of high explosives.

While most B-24s served in their primary role as heavy bombers, bristling with machine guns, flying on many of the worst missions in every theater of war, some B-24s were converted to photoreconnaissance aircraft. Others were used as tankers, flying cargoes of gasoline to feed the hungry engines of the Army; others were converted to transports, hauling personnel and supplies. Other B-24s, painted pitch-black, flew night missions, dropping agents into occupied territory by parachute.

Still other aircraft monitored the weather, dropped leaflets over enemy territory, or flew radio countermeasure missions. For both American and British air forces, the B-24 also served as an effective antisubmarine aircraft. Keen, versatile weapons, B-24s would drop more than 600,000 tons of bombs and shoot down more than 4,000 enemy aircraft in the Pacific theater of war.

Australia, the prize protected by the great arc of Papua, New Guinea, was 7,500 long miles from the west coast of the United States, 7,500 miles of trackless ocean and island airstrips, 7,500 miles of danger. Every bullet and can of rations, every soldier and marine, had to cover this long, risky path. Given the length of the supply line, and given the critical need for every plane and man in the Southwest Pacific, finding the cause of noncombat crashes was worth taking any chance — no matter how risky.

Even cannibals.

The struggle for New Guinea had been touch and go from the start. With the fall of Singapore and the Dutch East Indies, Nippon's road to northwest Australia became passable. The Australian base at Rabaul fell in January 1942, overrun by the same Japanese landing force that had taken Guam from the United States. Some of Rabaul's small garrison got clear of the island after a terrible march through the bush, but the great anchorage was now to be the major Japanese base in the Southwest Pacific.

Japanese forces at Rabaul were within reach of three vital bases along the resupply lines from America to Australia: Fiji, Samoa, and New Caledonia. General MacArthur saw the situation clearly: if the Allies were going to fight for Australia outside that country's own borders, there was only one place to do it. New Guinea's time had come.

Early in the morning of March 8, 1942, Japanese landing forces appeared out of the gloom of the Solomon Sea, coming ashore at Lae and Salamaua, small ports in the Gulf of Huon, a great curved inlet on the eastern end of New Guinea. Strikes by Allied sea- and land-based aircraft did substantial damage, but the Japanese consolidated their position, and were flying fighters into their newly captured airfields by the tenth of the month.

Now the Allies faced several tough questions: What would Japan do next? Was an invasion of Australia in the works? Or would the Japanese strike at New Caledonia and Fiji, cutting off Australia's supply line from the west? Was Port Moresby in immediate danger?

The Australian command guessed exactly what the Japanese were planning. Although the Japanese Navy urged an immediate offensive against Australia, that would have required a great many troops. The Japanese Army argued that the Empire instead should move to sever the Australians' umbilical cord to America. An offensive against Australia could be mounted later. It would not do, however, to leave a hostile base on the flank of the attack against New Caledonia and the other Allied stepping-stones. So it was decided: Port Moresby would have to be taken before anything else was done.

The Allies reacted. Australia diverted two full divisions, then at sea, to the defense of Australia herself. General Marshall sent two American divisions west as well. General MacArthur was ordered out of the doomed Philippines and named supreme commander of the Southwest Pacific.

By April 1942, reinforcements were trickling into Port Moresby, and American and Australian air strikes hammered repeatedly at Lae, Salamaua, and Rabaul. The Japanese responded, repeatedly striking at the American bases in New Guinea throughout the spring and summer. By mid-August, the Japanese had hit Port Moresby almost eighty times.

To the Allies' great relief, the Japanese made no early move on Port Moresby. Finally, however, the Japanese fleet moved from Rabaul. Their objective was obviously Port Moresby. The Allies moved to intercept.

The result was the Battle of the Coral Sea, fought on May 8, 1942, the first fleet engagement in naval history in which the opposing ships never saw one another. The Coral Sea was a draw, for all practical purposes, but it bought Port Moresby a little more time. In May, Australian reinforcements began to land in New Guinea and the Allies started constructing more airfields. Then, in June, came wonderful tidings from the central Pacific: on June 4, 1942, a badly outnumbered American carrier force fought and won the epic Battle of Midway. Adm. Raymond A. Spruance's shrewd gamble had destroyed four Japanese carriers and their irreplaceable veteran pilots. The United States had lost a single flattop.

Now the Allies could seriously consider offensive action. The first attack would be on the Solomons, with the landing of the marines on Guadalcanal and Tulagi on August 7, 1942. Meanwhile, in New Guinea, the Allies decided to take a step forward by establishing an airfield at Buna, about halfway up the bird's tailfeathers, midway between the feather's tip at Milne Bay and the Japanese footholds in the Gulf of Huon. The landing would have to wait, however, until after a successful attack on Guadalcanal.

But the Japanese moved first. Before July was over, they were ashore at Buna, and getting ready to advance on Port Moresby. They came over the Owen Stanleys, a range of knife-edged ridges and wild, tangled jungle, where the annual rainfall averages between two and three hundred inches per year, and sundown lasts all day. They came over the Kokoda Track, a murderous, winding trail over ground at an elevation of more that seven thousand feet. At one point, the track rose six thousand feet in less than twenty miles. Here, far above the steaming swamps and jungles of the lowlands, it could be bitter cold at night.

By July 20, 1942, the Japanese column confronted Australian light forces along the track. In spite of fierce Australian resistance, the Japanese gained ground. They took Kokoda from the outnumbered Australians in mid-August, and waited for reinforcements to move south, take Port Moresby, and push the Allies into the Solomon Sea.

The Japanese buildup at Buna progressed rapidly. Unit after

unit of reinforcements came ashore in spite of Allied air attacks — line troops, vehicles, engineers, and artillery. On August 26, 1942, the Japanese advance began, commanded by hard-driving Maj. Gen. Tomitaro Horii. The Japanese managed to drive back the outnumbered Australian force in bitter fighting along the Kokoda Track.

On November 19, 1942, the Allied command at Port Moresby combined the American 126th Infantry with the Australian command. The Americans were to take over the attack at a critical track junction, and they were itching to get into action. Some of these Americans told the Australian troops that they could "go home now," because the Americans "were here to clean things up." Such boasts were not only impolitic; they would prove to be dramatically unfounded.

The Allies' progress slowed; it was as much a result of the terrible, tangled terrain as it was the determined Japanese resistance. In spite of repeated attempts to break through, the Americans could not crack the Japanese defenses. In a wild seesaw of attack and counterattack, the Americans lost almost twenty percent of their strength. Though they were unaware of it at the time, the combined American and Allied forces were outnumbered by the Japanese.

Some progress was made, but at a terrible cost. Air strikes were some help, but the targets were hard to see in the dense scrub, and some bombs killed and wounded friendly troops. There was little artillery help, and no tank support at all. When an attempt was made to move tanks to the front, the Allies found that the only available barges were too small: they simply sank, taking the tanks with them. And even when more artillery was finally added, the attacks made little progress.

Conditions were hideous. Many of the attacking troops were perpetually wet. Weapons, full of muck from the swampy conditions, jammed continually. Although rifle oil was available, it had been shipped in large cans that were difficult to transport. The water ranged from knee-deep to ankle-deep, and visibility was generally very poor. Machine guns jammed because canvas ammo belts shrank because of the moisture; hand grenades failed to detonate, their fuses ruined by the humidity.

There was some success, but there were heavy casualties. Some Japanese positions were overrun, and the Americans captured ammunition, food, and medical supplies. They also captured a safe full of little rolls of Japanese writing paper. It looked like toilet paper to the Americans, who put it to that very use.

On the whole, Buna was a bloody and frustrating battleground. In two weeks, the Americans suffered almost five hundred battle casualties, not counting men who suffered from heat exhaustion and disease. The combined Allied force failed to break the Japanese line.

The next move was almost inevitable. Disturbed by unsubstantiated rumors that American troops outside Buna had thrown away their weapons and run, MacArthur replaced the American commander with Gen. Robert Eichelberger. Without even briefing the new commander on the situation, MacArthur sent him to Buna with these comforting words: "Go out there, Bob, and take Buna or don't come back alive."

Eichelberger found the situation better than he expected, but he was immediately prepared to ask for reinforcements, a request denied his predecessor. Many of the men attacking Buna were exhausted and sick. They looked, as an Army doctor put it, "like Christ off the Cross." Many of them had lost the will to advance. Eichelberger relieved several subordinate commanders, and began to lay plans for further advances.

The new push on Buna did not begin well. The infantry assault made some progress, but still could not break through. Nevertheless, there was much to be proud of. The Americans had fought very well. On that point, Eichelberger was content: MacArthur could stop worrying about the fighting spirit of his men.

Still, Buna fell on December 14, 1942, and the Americans

moved on a neighboring position called Cocoanut Grove, which was captured the next day. Part of the bloody campaign was over, but more remained to be done.

On December 18, the Allies began another push — this time from the south — toward the American forces at Buna. The attack was designed to trap the Japanese in an Allied pincers. This time the attackers were Australians, and this time they were led by armor. The offensive lasted through Christmas. On New Year's Day, 1943, the Australians and Americans attacked again.

In the first week of October 1942, the fortunes of Japan had been ascendant. In spite of Midway, Japan still dominated the East and much of the Pacific. She was poised to move south against Australia. But by New Year's Day, 1943, the tenor of the war had miraculously changed. The last Japanese resistance was crumbling around Buna. The U.S. Army and the Australians had destroyed any hope of the Japanese conquering New Guinea. U.S. Marines had conquered Guadalcanal, and Japan had taken terrible losses on both land and sea.

When darkness fell on the first day of 1943, most of the agony was over at Buna. On the following day, the Americans spotted numbers of Japanese trying to escape in small boats and on rafts. Some of them were even swimming. Artillery, machine guns, and air attacks finished most of them. The two most senior Japanese officers had sliced open their bellies in ritual suicide, and the Americans set about rooting out the last survivors.

It was over at Buna, but much work remained. The Sanananda Track to the south had to be cleared, and a fresh, well-conditioned American infantry regiment was sent in to do the job. Alongside the Australians, the Americans — including the veteran 127th Infantry — pushed on to the sea, destroying the last vestiges of Japanese resistance. By January 22, 1943, another two thousand Japanese were dead, and the booty was enormous: all manner of weapons and supplies; even motor vehicles bearing U.S. Army markings.

xi   Into Darkness

The agonizing New Guinea campaign was no sideshow: it was an important part of the greatest war ever fought. The men who fought there played a vital role in the Allied counteroffensive in the Pacific. The Allies methodically wrenched the huge island from Japan's dogged defenders. In January 1943, the Australians opened a forward base at Wau, in the mountains west of Salamaua. In June, American troops captured the Woodlark-Trobriand Island group north of the tip of the Papuan bird's tailfeathers. More airfields there would support still more air power, to hammer the Japanese positions along the north coast of New Guinea, Rabaul, and Kavieng.

As the story that is told in *Into Darkness* unfolded in the spring of 1943, the deliberate island-hopping campaign continued across the vastness of the South and Central Pacific. The enemy was still fanatic, still powerful. Every aircraft was worth its weight in gold, every man was irreplaceable, and Ed Imparato's mission was of enormous importance to the difficult job that remained.

In September 1943, American and Australian troops landed east of Lae, and American paratroopers dropped to the northwest, at a place called Nadzab. An Australian division was flown into Nadzab, and the move on Lae began. Lae and Salamaua fell before the end of September. In the first week of October, an amphibious assault carried Finschhafen at the northern tip of the Huon Gulf.

In January 1944, the Allies landed on the north coast of New Guinea at Saidor, and by mid-summer they occupied important points along the coast, all the way to the western tip of the island. Most of the Japanese defenders were dead. Those who remained were ineffective, starving fugitives wandering in the jungle of the interior.

The New Guinea campaign would prove to be a triumph of air, land, and sea cooperation. Air cover and air resupply played an essential role in the Allied victory. From difficult beginnings, from the early weeks when there was never enough food or medicine or ammunition, from savage firefights in impenetrable jungle where the combat was often hand-to-hand, from death by disease or exhaustion or friendly artillery and airstrikes — even from hastily organized expeditions to unearth a mystery in the heart of headhunter territory, the Allies had learned their trade and were on their way to triumph.

Col. Robert Barr Smith,
U.S. Army (Ret.)
Norman, Oklahoma

I
BRIEFING

This story begins at Port Moresby, New Guinea. The year is 1943. It was set in motion by a man who was always doing me favors, always concerning himself with my welfare — often to my great chagrin. I came to dread his interest in me, but I could not help liking him.

It was difficult to resist his backhanded way of saying, "Imparato, there's a job I want you to do." He was the boss, a lieutenant colonel, who had temporarily been placed in command of the troop carrier group of which I was a member. Our permanent commander had failed to return from a mission to Lae, one of the Japanese strongholds in New Guinea. His plane had been shot down by antiaircraft fire.

Replacing him in command was Lt. Col. Roger Beam, a nonrated officer. It was not the custom of the Army Air Corps to have an officer who was not an active flyer command a flying unit. But since Beam was the highest-ranking officer of the group, he automatically assumed command until higher headquarters could assign a flying officer as a replacement.

We anticipated that Colonel Beam would be replaced within a few weeks by another lieutenant colonel, a rated officer, but as the weeks dragged on, we wondered if the Army brass had forgotten our plight. Still, we hoped for change. Colonel Beam's nonrated status might seem an insignificant matter to some, but men are quick to sense that it might be easier for a commander to send crews out on hazardous missions when the commander himself does not have to expose himself to the enemy. And we were troubled by Beam's recklessness. Time and again his men had witnessed him needlessly exposing himself to Japanese planes during air raids. Colonel Beam would order his men into foxholes but, refusing to use the foxholes himself, he would remain in the open, glaring upward in defiance.

Assigning Beam as commander could either benefit or handicap his career. His successful exercise of command with this unit would increase his potential for promotion. His failure to run the group effectively would jeopardize his military future. This dilemma must have preyed on his mind. Beam had no way to show his leadership ability in the air under combat conditions as did other flying officers under his command. So he sought ways to demonstrate his bravado on the ground. He was an enigma, and yet he seemed to possess an underlying strength of character and empathy for his men.

One day in May 1943, I was lying on my GI cot at Port Moresby, having just begun to relax after returning from a difficult supply-drop mission. One of our planes was badly shot up and had to land at Bena Bena, our forward air strip. I closed my eyes to catch a few winks of sleep, which I had failed to get the night before. The Japanese had sent over an airplane to harass us, and we had hit the foxholes, wallowing for more than an hour in the mud that had accumulated from a heavy rain shower. Consequently, few men had slept that night.

A corporal poked his head into my tent.

"Major Imparato?"

"I'm Major Imparato," I said. "What can I do for you?"

"Sir, the Colonel wants to see you in his office right away," he answered.

"Okay, soldier. Tell him I'll be right over."

Once he was made temporary CO, Beam developed an uncanny ability to sense the moment I hit the sack for a rest. As soon as I undressed and stretched out, he would send for me. This seemed to be his method of showing me how indispensable I was as a group operations officer and pilot. By virtue of the fact that I was a major, I wasn't supposed to need sleep. That was for the lower ranks. Also, since I was older than most, I was supposed to have learned to endure the military's little hardships.

I hastily put on my clothes, figuring the sooner I got over to Beam's office the sooner I could come back and resume my nap. Of course this was wishful thinking. The ground was still soggy from the rain the night before, but I paid little attention to the sloshing, sucking sounds the mud made around my shoes as I walked, pondering what sort of deal Beam had cooked up for me this time.

I had once been called to his office merely to explain why I had split an infinitive in a piece of military correspondence that was being sent to headquarters. "I don't know an adjective from a proverb, Colonel," I had explained.

When I arrived at Beam's tent, he motioned me to a rickety chair near his polished mahogany desk. I had wondered many times where he had gotten the desk, since everything else in the outfit was makeshift and crude. Perhaps he had gone to great lengths to get this piece of furniture in order to enhance his prestige. He had ordered an enlisted man from the installations section to refinish it. The sergeant had done a beautiful job: the desktop was polished to a high gloss, not unlike expensive desks I had seen in the States.

Just as the colonel was about to begin, the field telephone rang. The conversation was one-sided and brief. He said a few "Yes, sir's" and "No, sir's," then, hanging up the phone, he slid his chair back, propped a GI-booted foot on the desktop and, as he lit a cigarette, gave me his "There's a job I want you to do" look.

"Impo," he said, "how'd you like to take a little walk?"

I didn't particularly like the nickname, "Impo," he had given me, but it was his prerogative. Had I asked him to call me "Ed," as everyone else in the unit did, I would only have aroused his ire and found myself saddled with even more of the "interest" he had already so graciously bestowed upon me.

Irked by being called Impo, I didn't answer him. Instead, I, too, lit a cigarette. This invitation sounded ominous. I looked at him, wondering what he had in mind, already opposing whatever it might be.

"I'm sure you're keeping my best interests in mind, Colonel," I finally answered.

"Just had a call from the general before you came in. He indicated that he has a job for you."

"Permanent or temporary?"

"Temporary."

So the general, the old man, was looking out for my interests too. That's what I liked about New Guinea. Everyone was always looking out for everyone else, except the poor guy at the bottom of the chain of command.

"Tell the old man I'm busy," I said. "Say I'm flying a mission or something."

Colonel Beam shot back quickly, "Tell him yourself."

He had me there; my back was once again against the wall. That was one of Beam's most insidious characteristics: he was quick to put you on the defensive. He often used this tactic to his advantage.

"Okay, since that's the way it is, let's have it," I said.
Beam dropped his feet off the desk, took out a drab olive GI handkerchief and mopped the sweat from his face. A long wisp of sand-colored hair, the only one on his nearly bald head, dropped down across his eyes. He pushed it aside. I had wondered many times why he continued to nurse that lonesome lock instead of cutting it off and ridding himself of the nuisance of having to continually wipe it back off his forehead.

"I don't know the details, Imparato, but the call I just got was from the general wondering why I haven't sent you to his office."

"Everything's a panic," I grumbled.

"Panic?" Beam asked, puzzled.

"Yes, panic," I repeated. "All I have to do is get back from a mission and hit the sack for a few winks and someone pushes the panic button. When I'm not flying I can lie around this rat hole for days and nothing happens. But just let me fly, let me come in dead tired like I am right now, and every dirty job in the unit is thrown directly at me."

"Who said this is a dirty job?"

"Aren't they all dirty in New Guinea? You got any clean ones in mind?"

"I know none of the details," he repeated, putting out his cigarette and lighting another one.

"I think you know more than you're telling."

"The old man said something about you taking a walk, a long one. That's all I know, except that you're late seeing him."

"You just told me about it. How could I be late?"

"You were late getting back from the mission."

"Colonel, we damned near lost a crew out there this morning, right in the face of heavy Jap ground fire, and I had to help escort the pilot to Bena Bena! You think I'm going to sit up there and do nothing to help a guy who's in trouble just because you think I ought to run back here and be your errand boy?"

"Now cool off, Impo, and get on over to the general's office. I'll go with you."

"Colonel, I'm dead tired. You don't have to fly missions. You don't understand how a man feels after he's lost a lot of sleep and had his fanny brushed by Jap bullets."

Colonel Beam was what we aviators called a "paddlefoot," the kind of flyer who does his buzzing behind a desk. Without first-hand experience, Beam looked at flying much as he looked at getting in a car and driving to the corner grocery; and delivering supplies to battle-weary American jungle troops who were pinned down by Japanese patrols was about as challenging as a delivery boy carrying goods on a bicycle.

To those of us who flew across the jungle day after day, seeing the American and Australian ground troops struggling with death, smelling rotting enemy corpses as we flew low over a battle area to drop supplies, flying meant something else. An aviator had to have a strong stomach in order to witness such horrors and still be able to eat, haunted all the while by thoughts of what he had seen.

Colonel Beam did not believe that men could be pushed too far or too vigorously. He considered flying a form of escapism, a method of running away from the torment men on the ground suffered when the Japanese delivered their rations of bombs and bullets. I was in no danger of breaking or being pushed too far, but there were those who were. Quite a few men went home without medals. All they had to show for their service were tight white jackets with handless sleeves tied in back.

"Colonel, whether the old man likes it or not, I'm going to take time to clean up. I can't go there looking like a bum."

"I won't argue your last point, but if you insist on being late, you'll have to answer to the general for it."

"Suits me," I said.

I got up from my chair, casually kicked it aside, loosened the front of my trousers and stuffed my shirt tail in deeper, trying to look more presentable. My shoes were covered with mud, and I hadn't brushed my teeth or shaved for almost twenty-four hours.

"The old man wouldn't want to see me looking like this," I said.

"I agree, Imparato."

"For once we agree on something," I muttered as I left his tent.

"I'll wait here for you," he called after me. "We'll go to the general's office together."

I wasn't surprised that he wanted to go along, since he was extremely inquisitive. I wondered if he wanted to be there to volunteer me for more favors should the occasion present itself. But what concerned me most was the "walk" the general wanted me to take. Brig. Gen. Ennis C. Whitehead, Commander, Advance Echelon, 5th Air Force, didn't know me personally. Our conversations had been limited to his "Good morning, Imparato," and my response of "Good morning, sir."

Slogging back through the mud toward my tent, I thought about what the general might have in mind. Had I spoken to him on the phone as Beam had, I would have probed a bit further. I would have at least found out whether my men were involved.

It took about twenty minutes to shave, shower, brush my teeth, and slide into a clean (but wrinkled) uniform. Even though I had used GI soap and scrubbed the uniform to rid it of the New Guinea grime, it already had the familiar musty, stale smell of the island. I walked back to Colonel Beam's office. He had just lit another cigarette and was puffing away, apparently revelling in some idea he had conjured up while watching the wreath of smoke curl about his face.

I did not dislike this man. In a way, I felt sorry for him. All he had to look forward to each day was making decisions on the ground and supervising their execution. He had less control over what went on in the air, and perhaps this was the reason he did not seem to care about his pilots and aircrews. An incident that occurred on a mission to Salamaua, another Japanese stronghold in New Guinea where we often flew in support of our ground troops, had led me to this conclusion.

I was part of a formation of three C-47 transports winging toward Salamaua. Overhead, twelve P-38 Lightning fighter planes zoomed back and forth, sweeping the skies clear of Japanese Zeros who might attempt to interfere with our mission. We reached the target area unmolested, made our drop on the designated area near our troops who were dug in fighting against Japanese patrols, and turned back toward Port Moresby. While we were over the target, the Japanese on the ground sniped at us, boring several bullet holes in the tail of my airplane. Aside from that, the drop mission was uneventful.

A few minutes away from the target we gunned our engines for the climb out back over the hills to Moresby. Lt. Bill Glenn, my copilot, had just gotten out of his seat to go back to the rear of the plane to stretch his legs. When he returned I would go back and do the same while Bill flew the C-47. He hadn't even reached the rear of the plane when a voice on the radio broke the stillness. I recognized the excitement in the voice of Thomas Lane, a young lieutenant.

"Major, I got an engine out!"

At the time we were flying barely five hundred feet above the ground in loose formation. I was leading, Lane was riding my left wing, and Lt. Carl Jones was on my right.

"Which one's dead, Lane?" I shouted into my microphone, at the same time motioning to my enlisted crew chief. Turning away from the mike I said to Sergeant Butler, "Get Glenn back up here fast."

"Left one. She's dead and she won't feather!"

If Lane couldn't successfully "feather" the dead engine, the propeller would windmill and cause heavy drag on the airplane, keeping the remaining engine from pulling the C-47 through the air at a speed high enough for Lane to climb over the hills between Salamaua and Port Moresby. I knew that Lane, flying an empty airplane, could remain aloft as long as the other engine performed properly, but what good would it do to stay in the sky when he obviously couldn't get across the mountains and back to base? Then I remembered Bena Bena, our forward airfield.

"I'll take the lead, Lane!" I directed. "Follow me!" I didn't want to tell him exactly where we were headed, because the Japanese were probably monitoring our frequency and might attempt to intercept our formation. I called the P-38 leader overhead and told him to stick close all the way. The Lightnings were flying high, circling and weaving back and forth in an effort to stay close to us. Our airspeed, because we had to lag back with Lane, had dropped off to a little under 120 miles per hour. Since the fighters were much faster than the transports, it was difficult for them to remain close to us. I could see them, the twin-engine, twin-boom fighters, circling gracefully overhead. It was a comforting feeling.

Slowly, I pulled out ahead of Lane while Jones brought up the rear, and we turned toward Bena Bena, an airfield near the north coast of New Guinea. Checking my map, I realized that Bena Bena was more than an hour away. Lane could make it if the right engine continued to run. There was a chance it wouldn't, but we had no choice — we had to continue on as far as the crippled bird could go and hope for the best.

After a few minutes, I called back to Lane. "How's she flying?" I asked.

"Fine so far," he answered. "Glad those fighters are up there."

"Likewise," I said.

I thought the conversation had ended but Lane came on the air again. "Major, why don't you and Jones head on back? Split up the fighters and let part of them go back with you. The rest can cover me."

"Shove it, Lane. We're all going together. Get that straight."

"Roger, Major. If that's the way you want it," Lane muttered.

Lane's voice seemed calmer. He was his old self again, composed and casual. That's what I liked about him, why he was completely dependable, why I liked to fly with him on the rough missions where a cool head was a man's ticket home. I had been in the same foxhole with him during an air raid on Port Moresby. Instead of panicking, Lane passed a box of hard candy around and made light of the fact that the Japanese were there trying to kill us. When the raid ended he climbed out of the foxhole, went back to his GI bunk, and napped as if nothing had happened.

When the conversation ended, the flight settled down to pure boredom. I propped my right foot on a pedestal and relaxed. I was just at the point of closing my eyes to give them a break from the glare of the New Guinea sun when I saw something streak past the cockpit. I sat up quickly and shuddered as I saw a Japanese

Zero make a sharp turn in front of me.

Grabbing my microphone I yelled, "Zero attacking us!" to the fighter leader flying high overhead. The Zero had snuck in completely unnoticed by flying fast and low. I yelled into the microphone again, this time to the transports, "Split up!"

I cut hard to the left and pointed the nose of my C-47 downward, slamming the throttles forward at the same time to get as much speed out of the bird as possible. At the moment I wasn't worried that I was quickly approaching the red line on the airspeed indicator, the point at which the transport's wings might rip off. I didn't care. It was worth the gamble to see if the red line actually meant anything; I had to push the plane's limits if I wanted to evade the Japanese fighter.

The Zero pilot made his turn and streaked back toward our formation. I watched Lane helplessly trying to nurse his airplane into a steep turn. The Japanese pilot sensed that something was wrong with Lane's transport. Ignoring Jones and me, he bored in on Lane. The first burst of machine gun fire caught the transport squarely in the cockpit. Metal splintered down the fuselage and fluttered away in the slipstream. The Japanese pilot, closing in fast and bent on the kill, pulled the trigger of his guns again. The bullets ripped into Lane's right wing and engine. The plane exploded into flames, leaving a horrible reddish blue trail along the length of the fuselage.

Bill Glenn reached over and gripped my arm. "My God, Major . . . look!"

I was looking. Every man in the remaining transports was looking. We watched as Lane's C-47 went into a long, steep dive, rolled over on the left wing, then righted itself. But it fell off on the wing again. The first burst of ammo into the cockpit had probably killed Lane and possibly Gibbs, his copilot, also. The plane was flying by itself now, performing strange maneuvers. With the left wing down, the plane spun out of control, a falling fireball. Seconds later it hit the ground and exploded in a wall of orange flame. One glance at the fiery holocaust below was sufficient to convince us that no one had survived.

Our grieving for the dead crew was short-lived, however. We were next on the Japanese pilot's list. Two unarmed airplanes against one heavily armed and fast Zero didn't have a chance. Our only hope was to get as close as possible to the treetops and stay there, to take advantage of every ravine and valley, especially those in our direction of flight. I wondered if we could dodge the Zero long enough to run him out of gasoline.

For the next few minutes I wouldn't have bet a penny on the lives of any of us. The other transport, piloted by Jones, was out of sight, but I knew it was still flying because I had Bill get him on the radio. Jones was performing the same kind of evasive maneuvers we were. We were so intent on dodging the Zero that we didn't realize it had been shot down by two P-38 pilots — too late to save Lane.

I climbed up a few hundred feet and made a circle, looking around for the Japanese pilot, ready to drop back down to treetop level at any second. I didn't see him, so I pulled up and climbed for altitude. Once I had reached three thousand feet, I saw Jones's airplane to my left. He, too, was climbing and flying toward Port Moresby. Then the fighters moved in close. Jones swung over and joined me, and when we parked the airplanes at Moresby and got out, my knees felt like they were made of rubber. None of us said anything. There was nothing to say. We were debriefed by the intelligence officer that afternoon and allowed to go to our tents.

The following morning I made the mistake of going to Colonel Beam's office to discuss something with him. In the course of our conversation, I mentioned the incident of the previous day in a manner which he might have interpreted as arrogant.

"Quit your bitching, Imparato. They're dead. You have to expect that kind of stuff in war. Forget about it."

Forget about it! Forget about a friend like Lane, a man with whom I had lived, eaten, and flown. Forget about the other men who were also my friends. Just like that. Wipe them from my mind and say to myself, "They never existed." They came from the soil and God has seen fit to put them back again. You'll die, too, Imparato, and people will forget about you the same day! So why worry about one insignificant crew? Will they be missed by more than a pathetic few? My thoughts were wild and I was bursting with anger.

"Like hell I'll forget it, Colonel!" I said. "You can stop a guy from committing an outward act, but you can't keep him from thinking."

"You're about to get out of line, Imparato."

"Out of line? For thinking about Lane and his boys? Yes, I guess you would call it being out of line." I moved closer to him. "Colonel Beam, there's just the two of us here. Now I want to tell you something: don't you ever again insult me about an incident like yesterday's. I suppose it's hard for you to understand about flying people and the friendship that develops among them. I hope the Good Lord will forgive you for what you said."

"I didn't mean it like it sounded, Imparato," he said, his voice sounding almost pathetic. His face was sallow and his jaws quivered from the cheekbones down to the corners of his mouth. "What I meant to say was . . ."

I didn't wait to hear the rest of his explanation. All I wanted to do was get outside into the clean air, out of the presence of this man who apparently had no compassion for men who had died in the line of duty.

I wanted to bash Beam's teeth in. I wanted to make him sorry he had ever come to New Guinea. But when I was alone outside, walking toward my tent, I realized that insubordination could bring my career to an abrupt halt should Beam decide to press charges.

When I returned to his office the following day, Colonel Beam was his old self again. Not once did he indicate that we had been at odds the previous day, but I could not forget what had been said. The matter was never mentioned or discussed again.

As I stood before his desk waiting for him to accompany me to the general's office, I thought of that incident, of his utter indifference toward Lane's death. Slowly, I felt my anger returning. Beam lit another cigarette from the butt of the one he had just finished and I lit one, too, hoping it would calm me down.

"Be with you in a second, Imparato," he said, sliding some papers into a drawer.

"It seems to me, Colonel, that you would at least have an inkling of what this business with the general is all about. I haven't done anything recently that would require the old man to pin a medal on me."

"No, he's already done that."

"I haven't been in any trouble and I certainly can't have charges hanging over my head."

"What are you so worried about, Imparato?"

"Nothing, except that when I'm about to face a general, I want to know, if possible, why I'm there. I'd like to go prepared."

"Well, this time you're going just as unprepared as I am. He wants you for some kind of walking job, that's all I know."

"Colonel, I'm a flyer! I thought that kind of duty was reserved for ground soldiers. Besides, right now I don't have the energy to sit down and get up again."

"Don't tell me about it, tell the . . ."

". . . General," I said, finishing the sentence for him.

"He's the one who picked you for the job."

"After who volunteered me?"

"I didn't volunteer you. The general sent for you personally this time." I didn't believe him.

Beam got up, tried to hide his little potbelly under his belt, and followed me out. We got into my jeep, pulled out onto the washboard road, and turned toward the general's office. Beam touched my arm.

"Go faster. We're already late."

"Maybe you haven't noticed, Colonel, but there's a pair of

MPs riding my tail."

It suddenly occurred to me that I might have a way out of this "long walk." Getting myself arrested and detained for speeding might delay the meeting with the general long enough for the old man to get disgusted and find himself another boy. But I wasn't thinking straight. It wouldn't be a good idea for a major in the Army Air Corps to get arrested in order to dodge his duty.

The general's headquarters was located about two hundred feet above the road on the crest of a small hill. We dismounted and stumbled up the steep steps. Even though I was much younger than Beam, I was puffing like a marathon runner at the end of a race when we reached the door to headquarters. Colonel Beam seemed about to collapse. We were both drenched with sweat.

General Whitehead's aide-de-camp, a young captain, sat at his desk in the outer office and motioned for us to sit down. It was then that I noticed that Colonel Beam and I were not alone. Four other officers, all of whom I knew well, sat quietly watching the aide-de-camp shuffle a huge stack of papers. Late as I was, I was relieved that the meeting had not started. I wasn't sure whether I was the reason for the delay. One glance at the others convinced me that I could have come in my other clothing. They all looked like second cousins to bums.

Capt. John McGovern, a man of about fifty, sat chewing on the end of a ragged cigar butt. The few remaining hairs on his head had already turned gray. I wondered how he had been picked to be sent to New Guinea when a younger man would have probably been more valuable. Mac, as he was known, had been a pilot in World War I and had credited himself with knocking down two German Fokkers with his Spad fighter. His face was weather-beaten and tough — it was obvious that he was an Army man through and through, although he was no longer a flyer, having been grounded many years before. Looking at him I thought, "If that old geezer can make it, so can you, Imparato."

Across the room from McGovern was Capt. Lewis Lock, a

B-24 bomber pilot whom I had known since the day I arrived in New Guinea. He was about twenty-four, and quite handsome with his thick black mustache and sturdy physique. He was the best rifle shot I had ever seen. I figured that Lock had been picked for this mysterious mission for a reason.

The third man in the group was Lt. Bill Brady, a wrestler type with a wonderful disposition. He was the kind of man who could give you a nice smile, then knock your teeth down your throat. Brady's temperament, not his huge, muscular physique, made him one of the most popular men at the base.

Lt. Paul Reed was nearly forty-five and looked even older than McGovern. Perhaps it was because he was so skinny. I wondered about his qualifications to perform whatever type of mission this was to be. I wondered if he didn't belong in a hospital bed instead of in combat.

I exchanged a few words with the men. The general's aide looked at me as if I were committing a mortal sin by making small talk while he was trying to work. Colonel Beam wasn't saying anything. He sat quietly nursing another cigarette. At the sound of a buzzer, the aide got up and left the room. A minute or so later he returned and said stiffly, "The General will see you now. Please come this way. You first, Major Imparato."

We walked into the old man's office in single file, with me in the lead, in our best military style. In my case, my best was none too good; and since I was leading the pack, the other men followed my sloppy example. We halted in front of the general's desk and I saluted. "Major Imparato and party reporting as ordered, sir," I blurted out.

The general returned my salute and motioned us toward his beautiful, huge, conference table. Ten straight-backed wooden chairs were spaced evenly around the table and a large map of the southwest Pacific hung on the wall. It was then that I noticed that Colonel Beam was not in the room. Apparently, the aide had passed the word to the general that Beam was there, and the general had asked the aide to detain him in the outer office.

A tall, gray-haired, distinguished-looking man, the general took a seat at the head of the table and told us to sit down. When we sat, he stood up and walked toward the wall map. A feeling of anxiety welled within me. Had this been a briefing for a flying mission, I am certain I would have felt no nervousness. I was never nervous until the mission actually began. We knew what to expect in a flying briefing, since flying missions had been routine for several months. But this time, I had no idea what to expect.

We watched the general gaze thoughtfully at the map. Finally, he turned to us.

"Gentlemen, in the past, we in this theater of war, and Air Corps in other theaters of war, have lost an occasional bomber through some cause which we know was not an enemy action. We are also reasonably certain that the losses were not due to weather. It is usually the case in such incidents that the bomber is never located, either having crashed at sea or somewhere in the jungle off the beaten path of our regular bombing and reconnaissance flights."

I shifted in my chair. Why was the old man telling us this? We often lost airplanes by accident and not by enemy action. Why were we so concerned about this now? It seemed more logical to concentrate on methods of keeping the enemy from shooting us down. The general continued.

"A few days ago another such mishap occurred which, as far as we know, was not due to enemy action. The fighters were up that day and swept the skies clean of Zeros.

"This bomber, according to reports, didn't have time to reach the target area before the crash occurred. We had a position from the pilot when he was about an hour out on course. About thirty minutes later, we learned that the bomber had crashed. I sent a plane to the area and the men were able to locate the wreckage from the air."

The general placed his finger on the map of New Guinea,

held it there for a moment, and then removed it. "That, gentlemen, is where the plane is. The search plane, a P-38 fighter, stayed over the wreckage for a considerable time looking for survivors, but from the pilot's report we are reasonably certain there were none. The plane was badly wrecked; in fact, part of it burned." He paused for a moment. "Are there any questions, gentlemen?"

I raised my hand. "Yes, sir. You've briefed us about what happened to the bomber, but just where do we fit into the picture?" The general smiled for the first time since the beginning of the briefing.

"I suppose that's quite an important question to you fellows. I became so engrossed in what I was saying that I forgot to mention the part you'll be playing in this mission. It's this: since we have lost several bombers due to unknown causes, we must attempt to determine the cause of this crash. You, Major Imparato, are maintenance qualified and a pilot. You will lead the group. Captain Lock is a bomber pilot, one of our best. He knows just about all there is to know about the B-24 Liberator. He's also a crack shot. You'll need him, Imparato, to do double duty."

I was beginning to get the gist of this meeting and I didn't like what I was hearing.

"As you can see, all of you have a particular qualification. Your job is to go as a team to that crash and attempt to determine the cause. You will leave as soon as possible — as soon as you can get your gear together. Major Imparato will be in charge from the time you leave until you return. And, gentlemen, I hope you all return safely. Are there any more questions?"

Again it was I who sat with raised hand at the general's invitation. Whitehead nodded and I got up and walked to the wall map. "General, would you mind pointing out that location again?"

He looked at me quizzically as if he wondered if I were about to give him an argument. "Why, no, Imparato." He pointed to the tiny spot again. "It's right here, about twenty-five miles from our forward airfield, Bena Bena."

Moving closer, I studied the map carefully for a moment. Then, as if something had suddenly exploded inside me, I said, "General, I'm a flyer, not a foot soldier!"

"So?" General Whitehead asked, a look of amazement on his face. "What's that got to do with it?"

"Well . . . nothing, sir, except that the crash lies right in the middle of uncontrolled territory. No white man has been there before."

"I know," the general said.

"But, sir, there are headhunters in there who'll eat you at the drop of a hat!"

The general smiled broadly and patted my shoulder. "Not me, Major Imparato — you!" he said.

II

PORT MORESBY

That was that. General Whitehead had spoken. And although I was sure he meant his last words in jest, the remark had disturbed me. There was no question that someone had to determine what was causing the mysterious crashes; I just wondered why it had to be me.

In war, people are called upon to perform duties which are not, strictly speaking, part of their job. It is impossible to train people for every situation that might arise. In war, and especially in combat, no one cares about job descriptions.

As I walked in the Papuan sunlight to the jeep where Colonel Beam sat waiting for me, I realized that I had been detailed a task, a fathomless task for which I had no experience and over which I had absolutely no control. I had been given many extra duties in my career, but this, without question, was the most challenging.

As we rode back to our quarters in silence, my thoughts returned to the day I reported for duty in New Guinea, the day I met Colonel Beam.

"Hotter than the fangs of hell" is an old Army expression. If ever I have felt Satan's hot breath engulf me, it was the day I stepped off the transport plane from Australia into the scalding New Guinea heat and saw for the first time what was to be my home for many months to come.

New Guinea, at first glance, was all I had heard it to be: searing tropical sun, flies by the millions, lush tropical growth, swamps, kunai grass, and high ragged mountains which seemed to be reaching to great heights just to escape the awful heat. I had read about this place in books, I had heard stories of gold mining and exploration; but the most accurate picture of this land had been painted for me by men who had fought here. And now I was here also, and I wasn't alone.

In addition to several thousand Americans and Australians, there was the enemy, the Japanese, a great number of whom were concentrated within seventeen miles of our base. From the stories that had reached us in Australia, it seemed that the Japanese were soundly pounding the Allies on all fronts. I did not doubt that they might at any time break through our defenses in New Guinea and chalk up another victory.

The Japanese had been in New Guinea longer than the Americans; therefore they had had ample time to dig in and prepare themselves for the fight. We were dug in too, in one tiny spot on the world's second largest island at a place called Port Moresby, only a stone's throw from the sea. To the front of our battle lines was the territory we needed to regain from the Japanese. To our rear was the sea. The Japanese wouldn't have to push far to drown us all.

Standing beside the empty airplane waiting for someone to come and meet me, I surveyed the air base. The sloppily placed tents were where the men lived and worked. Many of these American soldiers and airmen had probably come from swanky homes and apartments, from beautiful farms and country homes. Others had come from shabbier surroundings and were probably used to far less food than they were getting in New Guinea. But they were all on equal footing now.

They lived in the same tents and ate the same food. They cursed the Japanese with the same words and felt the same resentment toward the Army brass who had sent them here. They all dreamed about their wives and girlfriends back home, suffered the same emotional strains, and wore the same kind of clothing. No man was better off than any other. They were all subjected to the same raids and bombings by the enemy, and — most importantly — they were all at risk of being killed. No man was safe by virtue of his standing in the community back home; a man's wealth or political affiliation could not deflect the bullet or bomb that had his name on it.

Not once did I believe I would be killed in New Guinea. No man actually believes he will be killed in a war. It is always supposed to happen to the other fellow. Unfortunately, many a man has died believing right up until the end that it couldn't possibly happen to him.

Also, when one is young he is prone to concentrate more on his comfort than on his safety. I was no different. All I could see the first few seconds after unsteadily planting my feet on New Guinea soil was the mess and squalor in which I would have to learn to exist.

A man does not ever believe that a battle in which he is fighting will be lost. He prefers to believe that the proverbial miracle will save him from the jaws of death at the last moment. I suppose men have to believe this in order to wage war. A man has to have tremendous faith in himself or else he will be incapable of the level of bravery that combat requires.

As I stood there, growing more irked by the minute because I hadn't been met at the airplane, I realized that I didn't want to be leveled. Like all soldiers — and I'm afraid I disliked being called "soldier" since I was a pilot — I had a certain desire for travel and adventure, but this was asking too much. I wanted to do my traveling at my own expense and at my own convenience. I didn't mind paying for it. At the time, I didn't realize how high a price I would pay for adventure.

The more I waited, the more I wanted to get out of there, to go home, to forget the stinking war and all its problems and miseries. I realized I might be in New Guinea a long time and that it would be rough. But I was an officer, sworn to duty.

"Brace up, Imparato," I said to myself, knowing that was the only choice I had.

Even though I had been on the ground for less than five minutes, I already hated New Guinea with a passion I would never be able to explain. I hated it because it wasn't like the States, like home, like New York.

Much to my relief, I noticed someone walking in my direction. I had begun to think — and secretly hoped — I had come to the wrong place until the young, boyish-looking lieutenant extended his hand and asked, "Major Imparato?"

"I'm him," I said, realizing how nice it was to shake the hand of a fellow American. Although young-looking, the lieutenant carried himself like an experienced soldier. He had obviously seen his share of this land and its problems.

"My name's Lane, Thomas Lane," he said. "I'm assistant squadron operations officer. The commanding officer couldn't come because he's in a meeting with General Whitehead this afternoon. He asked me to see that you were taken care of."

I was relieved that the boss hadn't met me. I wanted to get used to the place on my own before meeting the CO.

"How long have you been in this hole?" I asked, trying to say it as pleasantly as I could. I knew it was going to be difficult for me to start out on the right foot.

"Ever since this mess started, Major — about six months."

"It's not a nice place."

"You'll get used to it. We all have. We don't like it . . . not as much as Australia anyway. No girls, Major," he said with a grin. "But I'll be going to Australia in a few weeks. Those Australian mamas had better lock their daughters inside."

I knew from that first moment I would like this boy. His countenance denoted stability, self-esteem, and realism. I also knew that if I stood talking to Lane in these unfamiliar surroundings much longer, I might be overwhelmed by self-pity.

"If you don't mind, Lane, I'd appreciate your showing me

where I'll be bunking down. I'd like to stretch out for a while. Mind giving me a hand with these bags?"

"Not at all, sir," he said, "but it's my guess you won't get much sleep in the daytime unless you have some way of keeping the flies and bugs off. Maybe I can get you a mosquito net a little later. The Japs hit us pretty hard yesterday and loused up part of the supply tent. Everything's in a mess over there." He pointed across the airstrip to a huge bomb crater. "It was one of their biggest raids."

"You have them often?"

"Almost every day, sometimes twice or more. It just depends on how the Japs are feeling and how badly our boys have beaten them."

"Looks like I'm in for a little fun during this tour."

"Yeah, Major," Lane said, his jaw tightening, "a lotta fun. It's real nice — just like the Fourth of July, except the sparks you see flying around are little red-hot pieces of metal that dig right into a guy's guts and spread him like butter all over the ground."

I patted his shoulder. "Come on, let's get me housed. We'll talk more later. You're going to have me so shaken up I won't be able to enjoy this island paradise."

Lane grinned with every muscle in his face. "We got no worries. Old Beam's taken care of that."

"Beam?"

"Yes, sir. He's acting CO until we get a new one. He's a paddlefoot through and through . . . thinks airplanes are an insignificant part of the Army. But as I was saying . . . the old man's got this bombing business all figured out. He's got foxholes dug all over the area and he's got some set aside for the officers and some for the enlisted men. I think the old boy figures that the Japanese wouldn't dare bomb the officers' foxholes."

"There are people like that. I saw them on maneuvers. But I never figured I'd see them in combat. A general I flew for once even took his house trailer out into the maneuvers area and pulled it right up beside the foxholes where the men were dug in."

"Seems a man like that is sort of optimistic."

"Or just plain stupid!"

"You'll learn about Colonel Beam soon enough, and I, for one, hope you can do something with him," Lane said, picking up one of my heavy bags while I shouldered the other one. We walked across the ramp to a battered jeep.

"I like to pass my own judgment on people," I advised Lane, knowing how easy it is for men to become prejudiced against whoever's in charge, whoever's making the tough decisions. Some people resent change. Perhaps Lane was one of them.

He drove me to a scattered group of tents and pulled up in front of one that was somewhat isolated from the rest. "This one's empty, Major. It might not be a very comforting thought, but the officers who lived here before didn't come back last week. That's why it's vacant now."

I got out of the jeep and looked inside the tent. It was gloomy in there. Three GI cots, devoid of blankets or pillows, sat at crazy angles to one another. The dirt floor was completely bare and the tent pole was adorned by a small, tattered pinup.

Lane stood in the doorway while I went inside and surveyed the tent as if it were a penthouse apartment I was considering buying. To say that the condition of my new home heightened my reluctance to remain in New Guinea would be an understatement. I caught a glimpse of Lane eyeing me, sizing me up, perhaps remembering the day he first walked into such a place.

"Just make yourself at home," Lane finally said, "and I'll trot over and see if I can scrounge some blankets and a pillow. We don't use sheets, here, you know."

I motioned to Lane with my hand without turning around, heard him gun the jeep engine and leave. I was alone again, and the emptiness I felt cannot be described in words. Walking over to the tent entrance, I looked out across the camp area. Several men were milling about.

I was "home." This was my house. I had three beds to choose

from. I selected the one nearest the door. Before lying down, I rolled up the sides of the tent to take advantage of whatever breeze might pass my way.

I lay down and closed my eyes. The heat was so intense that there was scarcely a dry stitch of clothing on me. I had nothing better to do than let my thoughts take over. There was a lot I needed to get off my chest. Perhaps, I thought, it would be better to admit to myself that I was unhappy.

"Imparato, you hate the damn place . . . you hate it!" It would be better to get it out of my system now than to subject whomever I met to a steady stream of griping. "That's it, Imparato," I told myself. "Get it out of your system now. Then walk out of this tent with the feeling that you've spent half your life here and wouldn't trade it for Saugerties, New York, or even New York City!"

My eyelids were heavy and I couldn't fight sleep. Gradually, I calmed down and a feeling of comfort came over me until I was barely conscious. It was a wonderful feeling, but the next instant a piercing wail shattered my peace. I had just fallen into the stupor that comes immediately prior to sound sleep; that part of drowsiness where one is neither asleep nor awake. I sat up on the cot, searching wildly around the dim tent. The high, ear-shattering note of a siren pierced the afternoon air. I had heard the sound many times in the States, where it only meant that a police car or an ambulance was passing by. This siren wailed mournfully. It seemed to be crying out for men who were about to die.

In my stupor I didn't know what to do. I got up slowly and put on the sweaty khakis I had taken off before lying down. That done, I put on my shoes, took out my comb, and combed my hair. All this time the siren continued to wail.

I suddenly was conscious of someone standing in the doorway of my tent. An enlisted man dressed in fatigues was looking at me. His face, smooth and hairless, indicated that he might still be in his teens.

"You the officer that just came in?" he asked in a twangy

Texan voice.

I nodded that I was.

"Well, sir, I don't know if it means anything to you or not, but we're 'bout to have an air raid out here a few minutes from now. I thought I might tell you about it in case you wanted to run."

"Run?"

"Yes, sir. No use staying here an' trying to be brave."

"Thanks," I said. "I appreciate you telling me."

"That's all right, Major. I just thought you'd like to know."

As the youngster disappeared, the siren wailed its last notes, the tone sliding down the octaves on what seemed a never-ending scale. The awful force of the boyish corporal's words finally hit me.

"AIR RAID!"

III

AIR RAID

Running outside, I searched for signs of other men heading for the air raid shelters, but I saw none. Only a few men appeared to be in a hurry, but even they were merely walking fast. Most of these men had been here for many months and had lost the sense of panic associated with air raids. They had settled into a routine; they knew what time of day a raid would take place, how long it would be after the siren sounded its warning before the Japanese planes approached the boundary of the airfield, and how many aircraft would attack.

I heard no airplane engines and saw no men running. I began to worry that the young airman had perpetrated a hoax and that I was the goat. Yet the siren had definitely gone off. No one would have sounded it unless it was the real thing.

Seeing the enlisted man who had warned me walking quickly a few yards away, I yelled at him. He turned and yelled back, "Come on, Major, 'fore you get your head blowed off." He pointed toward the hills. "They'll be coming from that direction in a minute or so." Needless to say, I followed him.

Moments later the airman dropped into a foxhole. I was still a number of yards behind him, puffing and blowing hard, wondering if I would be able to make it before the Japanese hit the airfield. I was sure they would like to catch some slow, ripe officer like me to use for target practice, but I was determined that they wouldn't catch me above ground.

While I was still several yards away from the foxhole, the

airman leaped back out and stood beside it, peering in. Again he jumped in and, just as quickly, popped back out. Then he bounced back into the hole and disappeared. I reached the edge of the foxhole and poised myself to drop into it when something hit me in the chest with such force that I lost my balance and fell backward. Picking myself up, I scrambled into the hole quickly, more concerned about my safety than about getting an explanation. A huge iguana, wobbly and weak — but still alive — crawled away from the foxhole. The boy had dropped into the hole smack on top of the reptile, which is why he had jumped out. When he had figured out what it was, he had grasped it by the tail and flung it out without looking up.

Peeping above the foxhole and seeing what he had done to an officer, the enlisted man looked uneasy and embarrassed. I'm sure he would gladly have faced Japanese guns rather than me at that moment. I crouched in the foxhole beside him.

"S-s-sir," he stammered, "I didn't . . ."

I couldn't help laughing, despite the fact that we were in the middle of an air raid. I felt the muscle in his arm. "Young fellow, you must be a second cousin to Dizzy Dean, the way you slammed that creature into me."

"Sir, I didn't mean . . ."

"The heck you didn't. I could tell that you did it on purpose. I heard that the CO has separate foxholes for the officers and enlisted men. Could be you didn't want me infringing on the airmen's territory," I kidded. The boy's expression didn't change. "Tell me, Corporal, did the old . . . did the CO actually do that? I mean, does he make the officers and men use different foxholes?"

The boy's face relaxed and returned to normal. He rubbed his fingers together for a moment, a nervous habit. "I'm afraid it is, sir. You see, he's a mighty peculiar man."

"Peculiar?"

"He sure is . . . mighty peculiar. Major, he never gets into a foxhole. He just sits and yells, 'No damn Jap's going to chase me underground! I'm not crawling into a hole like a rat!'"

"Sounds like he's more than peculiar," I said.

"He's peculiar, but he's brave," the corporal continued.

"A man can be brave and still get his tail shot off," I warned. Colonel Beam's bravery sounded superficial to me. I didn't think he was fooling anyone. What kept him from grabbing a foxhole like everyone else and cowering when the enemy cut loose with machine guns and antipersonnel bombs was probably ego; he was trying to appear courageous in the eyes of his men.

"Get a load of the old man," he wanted them to say. "It takes guts to do a thing like that. The whole damn Jap Air Force can't drive him into a hole!"

But if this was Beam's reasoning, it was wrong as far as I was concerned. Should the rest of the men in the group follow his example, standing at the perimeter thumbing their noses at the Japanese as they passed overhead, the enemy's job would be a simple one. It would only be a matter of picking them off one by one until the last man lay on his back in a pool of blood. I'm sure the Japanese would have liked nothing better.

"Yep, the old man's mighty peculiar, sir," the airman chuckled. "Funny thing happened one day, though. They durn near got him. He was standing close to a foxhole with bombs going off and the men yellin' fer him to get inside. But he wouldn't do it. He just stood there with a string of rosary beads talking to himself and sliding them beads as fast as he could. Maybe they helped, I don't know. But he wasn't killed."

I grinned at that too, wondering how a man could be naive enough to believe that prayer could stop bullets fired by a man willing to die for his power-crazed emperor. Colonel Beam, if he lived, would be the subject of tall tales for years to come. "How long will it be until the Japs get here?" I asked, remembering the danger we were in.

"Any time now. It varies. Sometimes they're here almost by the time the siren blows. That's when it's dangerous . . . don't give us time to get to the holes. Other times it's several minutes . . . like now . . . they shoulda been here. We got some fighters in the air that ought to be coming back soon. The Japs try to plan their attacks for when our fighters are up. They attack the field about the time they know our fighters are ready to come back low on gas. Our boys can't do much fightin' back and sometimes they can't land on the strip because of bomb holes."

"Many men killed in these raids?"

"You kiddin', Major? Hell yes, they get killed! Not always, but sometimes."

"That was sort of a stupid question, wasn't it?" I ventured.

The youngster answered me plainly. "Yes, sir, I reckon it was." I smothered my grin at his frankness.

My ears caught a familiar note in the air, the sound of an airplane engine. The enlisted man heard it, too. "Here they come, Major. Get as far down in this here hole as you can and stay there. Don't look up for nothin' or you're liable t'get your head blowed off."

He didn't have to tell me to stay down. I was already crouched against the side of the foxhole, my face digging into the hard dirt. I could hear the high-pitched whine of the enemy airplane clearly. I would learn to dread that noise — the sound of the Mitsubishi Zero, the sleek, single-engine fighter that could out-turn and out-maneuver anything we put in the skies against it.

I could feel my body trembling. The first bomb hit close by, sending a shower of dirt into the hole. WHAM! "Oh God!" I heard the enlisted man whisper. WHAM! Another one fell close by. The explosion was followed by a series of wild yells from men in the holes. There was no way of knowing whether or not the men had been hurt or had yelled in anger. WHAM! Another bomb landed farther away this time and I relaxed somewhat, thinking the raid might be over. The corporal relaxed too, and sat on the floor of the hole clutching his hands around his knees. I stood up, peered above the edge of the hole, trying to see what had happened to the airfield and the people, but I didn't get a chance. The enlisted man grabbed my belt and pulled hard. This time when he spoke there was a note of authority in his voice.

"Get the hell down, Major, if you want to stay alive."

I didn't argue. Letting my legs go limp, I collapsed on the floor of the foxhole; it was none too soon. A formation of planes swept in, machine guns chattering, and I could hear the bullets thudding into the ground and into the planes which were parked close by.

"Thanks, fellow. That was too close."

"Unless you're careful here, sir, you'll lose your cotton-pickin' head. Regardless of what Colonel Beam thinks about airmen not being able to sweat out a raid in a foxhole with officers, them Japs don't know no difference when they come over. You got to stay low until it's over."

The Japanese came over again strafing, this time shooting at another target. I was surprised that no more bombs were dropped. "This is a little one," the corporal explained. "The last time I thought they'd sent over half the Jap Air Force. They'll be back, though. They always make several passes from most every angle."

Sitting there wondering how long they would continue to harass us, I heard another sound on the airfield. Four American fighters — two P-40 Warhawks and two P-39 Airacobras — rolled into takeoff position. The pilots, evidently tired of waiting, were going up after the intruders. They didn't take time to warm up their engines. They rammed the throttles open and smoke streaming from the hot exhaust stacks wafted over the foxholes. It was a familiar smell and a good one. I imagined that the powerful Allison engines were actually screaming in defiance at the Japanese, daring them to fight.

It took real guts for those four pilots to go up after a swarm of Zeros, knowing that the Zero was a better plane. These American fighter pilots, for the most part, knew nothing of war except what had been explained to them during maneuvers in Louisiana and

South Carolina. The Japanese pilots, on the other hand, had been exposed to blood baths in the battles over China, where hundreds of innocent Chinese were killed. These experienced pilots, having tasted blood before, were eager to taste it again.

After what the corporal had told me about staying down, I made no attempt to see what direction our fighters had flown in. I only knew that four brave men, each probably no older than the man sitting next to me in the foxhole, had flown off to engage the Japanese. The Zeros did not return to continue their strafing attack on the airfield. Although we could not see it, we could hear the aerial battle. After a furious few minutes, the sounds of fighters approached the field, their engines popping with throttles cut back to land. The corporal poked his head over the edge of the hole.

"It's safe now," he said. "But it's happened again."

"What's happened?"

He pointed toward the oncoming planes. Only two were in sight. "That's the way it's been for a long time. They always seem to get a few of our boys."

I gulped at his remark. A flight of four planes goes out to attack the enemy and only two return. A loss of fifty percent was not acceptable. Many times, I was to learn, some of the downed American pilots were able to return to the base, having eluded the enemy by infiltrating their lines, but these two pilots would never return.

For the first time the full force of the war hit me. Although I hadn't seen it happen, I knew that within a few short, furious minutes, several men — both Japanese and American — had died. They had died violently, spinning to the earth in flaming airplanes.

There is a tendency for men in war to believe that the enemy is vicious, ruthless, inhuman; even uncivilized, heartless, and soulless. Each man believes that God is on his side. In those first few minutes in New Guinea, I found that attitude developing in myself. Maybe it was the strafing that had kept me pinned down like a reptile; maybe it was the vicious propaganda of Tokyo Rose;

maybe it was the newsreels of Japanese atrocities I had seen back home; maybe it was the loss of two of our pilots; maybe it was just my nature. At that moment I wanted to be vicious and heartless too.

With the battle over, I climbed out of the foxhole to go back to my tent and pick up where I had left off with my daydreaming and napping. It was quiet now that the fighters' engines had stopped. The screaming of the wounded I had expected after the raid never came, so maybe the Japanese hadn't done much damage this time. I walked back toward my tent slowly, followed by the young airman. No need to hurry, I thought; no need to do anything today in the way of settling into my new job; that could all wait until tomorrow. I had been through my first air raid and I had escaped alive.

We passed an empty foxhole with a small stain of blood near its edge. Someone must have been injured; how badly I didn't know. And there we stood when the lone Japanese Zero streaked in from the south. He had played a cagey one on us. The Zero blasted away with all guns as I yelled to the young corporal, "Hit the foxhole!"

I leaped in as the bullets rained overhead, splattering in the dirt. The Zero was gone in seconds and it was deathly quiet again. Poking my head above the edge of the foxhole, I cringed at what I saw. I leaped out and ran to the sprawled body. The dead man's blood had already stained his fatigues. Turning over the body and looking at the smooth, boyish face of the young airman who had saved my life only a few minutes before, I realized that I didn't even know his name.

IV
PREPARATIONS

It hadn't been a good night. I slept poorly, awoke early, and headed for the jeep we would use to take us to the airstrip. I stood beside the vehicle, waiting for the rest of the men in my party to catch up. We had to make plans about when we would begin the mission into uncontrolled territory, what kind of equipment we would take along, and how we would go about procuring native guides to lead us on our journey.

A few paces away from the jeep, where the ground was flat and sandy, I picked up a short stick, sharpened the point with my pocketknife, and was about to scratch some letters in the ground when Lewis Lock came up behind me.

"What're you doing, Ed?" he asked.

"Huh? Oh, I dunno." I had intended to write something but hadn't realized until that very second what it was. "I was about to write something," I said. "My epitaph."

"You gone nuts?"

"No, I haven't gone nuts. Think about what the old man said and you'll understand why an epitaph might be appropriate."

"You're a pessimist."

"I've got a right to be. I've been flying missions in the face of the Japs for months, taking everything they can throw at me. Just when I've got 'em outmaneuvered, when I've finally got everything under control, look what happens: the old man makes a paddlefoot out of me. He takes me off pilot status to send me chasing after headhunters. Now I ask you, did I join the Army for this?"

Lock laughed out loud. "I was thinking the same thing, Ed. What kind of war is this?"

Brady, great, powerful Brady, strolled up kicking sand innocently with his huge feet. "You asking me or Major Imparato, Lock?"

"I was asking Major Imparato, but if you've got the answer, we'll listen."

I looked at Brady, this powerfully built lad, and was glad we had him along. "I sure haven't got the answer," I said. "All I know is that all five of us are in the same boat. We're about to do a job we weren't trained to do. No one ever told us we might be called upon for this kind of duty. It's a screwy war."

"Go ahead," Lock reminded me. "Finish your epitaph. Let's see what it looks like."

I squatted down and brushed some small stones from the sandy area with my hand. With the pointed stick I scratched, "Here lies Edward T. Imparato."

"Is that all?" Brady asked.

"Let me finish."

I scratched several more words in the sand. The epitaph read: "Here lies Edward T. Imparato, who died, in addition to his other duties."

"Some joke," Lock said.

"I didn't mean it to be funny, Lew. It's the only gesture I could think of."

"It ain't funny, Major," Brady said. "You could substitute any of our names there. You might be happy about this assignment, but I'm not. I want you to know from the very start that I didn't volunteer for this. I'll go because it's an order, but I'm not happy about it."

I looked up at Brady, tall, stately, young, and obviously able. "I didn't pick you for the job," I said. "I was the last one told about the trip, and the last one to get to the meeting. The first I knew about it was when Colonel Beam told me."

I wondered why Brady had suddenly taken this attitude. He

wasn't easily intimidated. Of all the people I knew in New Guinea, I would have thought he would be the first in line should the call go out for volunteers for such an important mission.

"I know you didn't pick me," Brady said defiantly.

"Then what's bothering you? If you feel that way about going, why don't you register a formal complaint?"

Brady shifted his huge feet uneasily. "I guess because I wouldn't stand a chance of getting out of it."

"Why do you want out?"

"I'm due to leave for Australia in three days. Going over on the regular shuttle. I got a girl in Brisbane I'd planned to see."

"So that's it. Don't you think she could wait for a few more days? You'd have something to talk to her about when we get back."

"Who wants to talk?"

"You got me there. I've got a girl back home I haven't seen in a long time. McGovern and Reed both have wives. How do you think they feel?"

"I know they have their problems too, but I can do something about mine if I get to Australia."

I laughed out loud because he had a point. Lock laughed too. And then Brady grinned. "Okay, Major, this is the last time I'll gripe until the trip is over, providing you do one thing for me."

"What's that?"

"See that I get on the next shuttle to Australia after we get back."

"You'll be on it, rest assured," I said. "I'll fix it with the old man."

"Now, Lock, have you got a gripe?" I kidded. "If you do, speak your piece."

"No," he answered solemnly. "I'm not anxious to go either, but if I can take old Betsy along, I'll go willingly."

"No women on this trip. When did you latch onto a Mary, anyway?"

"Old Betsy's a gun . . . my rifle, the best friend I ever had."

"S'cuse me. I thought you'd latched onto one of the native women that hang around the camp."

"They're looking better all the time," Lock said, grinning.

"You got rocks in your head. Now let's get this straight. There isn't a man among us who wants to go. If we had our choice we'd take our chances against the Japs, but we haven't got a choice. Old 'Spit and Polish' has spoken and we are at his command. So let's make the best of it. You with me?"

They nodded. Reed and McGovern sidled up to the group. "How about you two? Got any gripes about going on this safari?"

They both shook their heads. "None," McGovern said. The old man wants it this way so that's the way it'll be. I learned to take orders a long time ago, back in World War I, in fact."

"This old geezer might admit to being that old, but not me," Reed said. "But he's right. Orders are orders."

"Okay, then. Let's consider this the final morale briefing and go along like the old man wants us to. If we expect to make this a successful mission we have to stick together. Anyone who gripes about it from here on is working for the enemy, as far as I'm concerned."

"We're all with you, Ed," Lock emphasized. "The only gripe we have is with the Army for sending us."

"Someone has to go."

"Yeah, someone has to go — us. And if the Army told us to swim to Australia, we'd have to do that, too."

"I'm all for it," Brady said, laughing. "Just say the word."

As we were readying to depart for Bena Bena, Colonel Beam approached me with his hand outstretched. "Let me shake hands with an old bushwhacker," he said in a voice that could have been interpreted as being sarcastic. For once, however, he was trying to be humorous, an unusual gesture for him. As soon as we shook, he drew back his hand as quickly as he had extended it and adopted his familiar scowl. "I suppose you know what this does to my outfit, Impo?"

"I'm not certain that I do."

"With you, McGovern, Reed, and Brady gone, I'll be in a bad way. You're the only operations officer I've got. Who's going to handle your job while you're gone? Have you thought about a temporary replacement?"

"Replacement?"

"Certainly. You may be gone a long time. Someone will have to do your job, plan the flights."

Of all the ridiculous things I had ever heard, this iced the cake. "Colonel, things have moved so fast I haven't had time to think about a replacement. Just do the best you can."

It was obvious that Colonel Beam didn't like what I had said.

"All right," he said. "I'll take care of it. We'll have to get along without you. Just get back as soon as you can."

Just like that, I thought, mentally snapping my fingers. Get back as soon as you can. As if I had any control over what would happen to us once we were in uncontrolled territory. Colonel Beam spoke to me as if I was going for a casual sojourn or a hike in the woods.

Although the officers who were to accompany me were all topnotch men, there wasn't a man among us with infantry experience. In aerial combat if we weren't crippled or forced into a crash landing, we could always race home, patch up the holes in our airplanes, fill our hungry bellies, rest, and be ready to fly again within a few hours. Fighting on the ground was different.

Life for a dogface soldier in New Guinea was as close to hell as a living man could get. Army brass and newspapers said the infantry had been trained for it. Perhaps they had. Perhaps the maneuvers in Louisiana had been sufficient training, but there were no Japanese in Louisiana. It's impossible to train a man for the sort of stress he faced in New Guinea. His body may adjust to the rain and mud; he may learn to tolerate the bites and stings of mosquitoes and sucking leeches; he may learn to go without food for so long that his stomach feels useless; but he can't learn all that in training.

The adaptation of the mind is another story. That's where I knew the dogface infantryman had the advantage over me. I knew nothing about the rigors of ground combat, the discomfort, the mental anguish, and the starvation.

"I'll be thinking about you, Impo," Colonel Beam said as we saluted, his voice softer than usual. "Take care of yourself."

When I looked back at him I could have sworn that his eyes had grown moist. He dipped into his pocket, removed his handkerchief, and wiped at his nose. "Take care of yourself, Impo, and the good Lord be with you," he shouted.

"Thanks, Colonel."

V
OUTPOST BENA BENA

On the way back to my tent after the meeting with the general, I ran into an Australian named Gil Timms, a liaison officer. Timms was a civilian who had spent fifteen years in New Guinea working in the Wau and Bulolo gold mines, so he knew that part of the island well. Timms was about forty-five years old, tall, and wiry. His features were plain, but his skin looked as tough as whet leather and was about the same color. He would be a good man to have along on this trek. Although the general had picked five of our team personally, he had never said we couldn't ask others to join the party. Gil Timms had an excellent command of Pidgin English, knew the bush and the natives well — at least those in controlled territory — and would be invaluable to me.

Timms was pleasant and jovial, a man with a quirky Australian sense of humor. He wasn't married; he had chosen life in the gold mines and combat over marriage. Dressed in wrinkled khaki clothing and wearing his hat pushed back off his forehead in the Australian style, he looked like the typical Anzac.

I briefly explained our mission to him and told him how important General Whitehead considered it. "Ed, you'd better take along some GIs," he said when I finished my pitch.

"GIs? That shouldn't be any problem. We have GIs here all the time."

Timms grinned. "I'm talking about shoes, Major."

Then I realized my mistake. The Aussies had certain expressions that I could never quite get used to. Timms enjoyed this play on words. "Oh, I see," I said, throwing some friendly sarcasm at him. "Why don't you Aussies say what you mean?"

"I might ask you the same, Yank!"

Timms placed a bony hand on my shoulder. "Sure, I'll go with you, Ed, if you can get the general's permission. I think I'd enjoy the jaunt."

"Okay, Gil. I'll check with the old man. I suppose you know I'm placing responsibility for my skin on your shoulders in this venture."

Grinning from ear to ear, Timms responded with an expression he knew a Yank could understand. "Well, now, Ed, I consider that downright neighborly of you!"

I knew that with Timms along the trip would at least be lively. In all probability it would be he who would help keep the group together when the going got rough. There was no question in my mind that this would be the most difficult mission of my military career.

I left Timms at my tent while I went to the orderly room to call General Whitehead on the field telephone. After quizzing me about the purpose of my call, the general's aide said the general would speak with me.

"General, this is Imparato. I'd like permission to take Timms along with me."

I thought I heard an explosion at the other end of the line. "I don't give a damn who or how many people you take!" the general shouted. "Just get that job done and report back to me!"

I heard a dial tone before I could even mumble, "Yes, sir."

Timms was with us as we straggled out to the flight line with our gear. We were taking along sleeping bags, guns, food, extra clothing, and boxes of goods to trade with the natives.

We were headed for a spot about seventy-five miles inland from the north coast of New Guinea. The natives in this region rarely got to the sea, so they valued things that one could only find on the coast. Timms advised us that New Guinea natives, especially the inland natives, prized salt above all else. They usually saved salt for feast days, weddings, and other celebrations. When all else failed, the use of salt would usually conclude a trading session in our favor. It could also be used to pacify hostile natives or to obtain information. In addition to salt, we were loaded down with *cuma-cuma* shells and *bari-bari* shells, which the natives used to make necklaces, bracelets, and other pieces of ceremonial decoration. We also brought knives, a dangerous but valuable trade item, to negotiate with the most difficult and stubborn traders.

We loaded our supplies aboard the C-47 transport and came back a final time to shake hands with some of the men who had assembled to see us off. Colonel Beam was still there, standing quietly off to one side in the semidarkness. I walked over to him.

"How many fighters are escorting us today?" I asked.

"Fighters? There won't be any fighters."

"No fighters? Colonel, one unarmed transport out there hasn't got a chance! You know that?"

"As well as you do, Impo. I asked about an escort and was cut off short. General Whitehead said the fighters are all out on a bomber sweep or covering our drop at Salamaua."

"So he considers us expendable."

"As he put it, the fighters covering the big sweep are performing a more important mission. There's more at stake than just one transport."

"At the briefing yesterday he seemed to indicate that this was the most important mission he had laid on for awhile. I was led to believe this was A-1 priority."

"Maybe he's changed his mind. At any rate, he's committed the fighters to the sweep and you'll have to go alone. I'm sorry. I tried to get a couple of fighters but the answer was a flat 'no.'"

"Well, that's that," I grumbled. We'll need all the luck we can get today." I stuck out my hand. "So long, Colonel. Hold things down around here."

"I'll do that, Impo. Good luck."

Good luck. His words were still ringing in my ears when I got on the airplane. Luck in a card game is one thing; luck in a sky full of Japanese Zeros is another. We needed the grace of God and His protection if we were to come out of this alive, I thought as I strapped myself into the bucket seat. At first, I had believed the only danger we faced was headhunters, but without an escort, we had to worry about the Zeros, too.

I couldn't help thinking about Thomas Lane and the day a Zero blasted him and his unarmed transport out of the sky. Japanese intelligence was sure to have learned about today's big sweep and they would be flying in swarms to counter it. I wasn't naive enough to believe they'd ignore an unarmed transport in order to concentrate on the big formations. They would try to shoot down everything in sight, and we stood a good chance of being one of the victims.

I didn't say anything about the lack of fighter escort to the others as we sat waiting inside the dark airplane. Instead I meditated, and even prayed a little, hoping that we would at least come through this part of the mission unscathed. The two pilots, both of whom were in my outfit, got in and walked toward the cockpit, stumbling over our feet in the semidarkness. Looking out the window I could see the hilltops in the distance faintly outlined against the sky. By the time the pilots returned to the base, huge clouds would have formed over the Owen Stanley Ridge. They would either have to skirt them or climb high to avoid the sudden up- and downdrafts associated with the buildups over the mountains. I had battled them many times myself and knew it was no picnic.

On this day, however, the clouds and bad weather might be an advantage for the transport crew. The clouds would provide a place to hide if the Zeros suddenly attacked. Any pilot would prefer a rough thunderstorm to an attacking Zero.

As the pilot started the engines, the smell of the acrid smoke drifted in through the little ventilation holes in the side windows. (These portholes were large enough to accommodate small arms or a rifle barrel and could be used for defensive purposes against enemy aircraft and enemy ground forces.) I can't explain it, but there is something about the smell of an airplane engine starting that always sends a thrill through me. The pilot revved up the engines and let them warm up until the cylinder head and oil temperatures were in the green. He taxied out onto the airstrip, hesitated for a few moments, then opened the throttles. The airplane moved along slowly at first, then gradually gained momentum, and a few seconds later, I felt it leave the ground. From the cockpit I heard the pilot yell, "Gear up!" It was strange to be a passenger in the rear of the transport. On all my flights in New Guinea I had been in the pilot's seat. Our pilots were good and I knew it, having flown with them, but as we climbed out and made a steep turn to the right, I couldn't help feeling a certain anxiety because I wasn't the one at the controls.

Realizing that the men in the cockpit wanted to live as much as the rest of us did, I settled into the bucket seat and tried to relax. No matter how I tried, though, I couldn't stop thinking about not having fighter escort for this mission.

After the pilot leveled off, I went over and sat down beside Gil Timms. He had closed his eyes and appeared perfectly relaxed.

"Gil." I touched his knee.

"Huh? Oh, yes, Ed."

"Gil, I have something to tell you that you won't like."

"I don't like a lot of things," he retorted.

"Well, you'll probably like this even less," I told him. "Did you know that we don't . . ."

". . . have a fighter escort?" he finished. "Of course I knew it, Ed. I didn't hear a single engine rev up besides our own. It wasn't too hard to figure out."

"And it doesn't bother you?"

"Not much, I've been exposed to a lot of danger since the Japs came to New Guinea. I've come to expect the worst even though I hope for the best."

"Are you bloody Aussies afraid of anything?"

"Afraid? Certainly we're afraid. We're as human as you Americans are. I suppose we just have a slightly different outlook on life. At least we look at New Guinea differently. You see, Ed, New Guinea is an Australian mandate, this part of it is, anyway. When the Japs moved in and tried to take it, they were, as far as we were concerned, trying to take part of Australia. I'm fighting for my own land, New Guinea though it may be, just as you would fight for Hawaii or Alaska. You understand that, right?"

Did I understand it? I had certainly never thought of New Guinea as a homeland for anyone but the black natives. But now Timms's feelings about this land and its people made sense. He was a part of it just as the natives were. Most of his adult life had been spent here. It was all he knew. Whether or not he was a native of New Guinea made little difference. He was as much a part of the land as if he had been born there.

"You make it easy to understand," I said. I had always looked upon the Anzacs as super soldiers because of the image they displayed. It had never occurred to me that the Aussies were fighting against an enemy bent on wresting from them what they considered to be their own land. Now I viewed Timms and the other Australians in a different light.

"Do you think we should tell the others about the escort?" Timms asked.

"Do you think it will serve any purpose?"

"Who knows?" he said.

I yelled out in the growing light, "I suppose you know we're alone this morning. There's no escort."

For a second there was a blank expression on Brady's face. Then he nodded. "Thanks for the heartening news. You couldn't have said a nicer thing before breakfast," he said glumly. The others didn't say anything. They looked at me and nodded, then closed their eyes again to try to grab a few winks before landing at Bena Bena. The mountains and almost two hundred and fifty miles separated us from our destination.

At ten thousand feet the airplane flew smoothly. There were no clouds over the mountains at that early hour. I looked at the ragged peaks and wondered what was happening down there. I was sure the Japanese had not occupied that part of the country, preferring to stay where they could use the automotive equipment they had brought to New Guinea. The mountainous terrain was practically impassable, even to those who desired to travel afoot. Only a native could adapt himself to that part of New Guinea, I thought.

Unfortunately, the good weather was short-lived. As soon as we crossed the mountains, we could see bad weather ahead. The pilot dropped almost to the tops of the low hills to avoid the buildup, hoping to get under the clouds and fly by visual reference to the ground. I went to the cockpit, thinking that another pair of eyes might help.

The pilot began zigzagging in and out of ravines, climbing over jutting knolls, gunning the engines to clear the peaks. While I was standing between the two pilots in the cockpit, we came face to face with a jagged crest that seemed to be reaching out to grab at the wings. The pilot racked the plane over in a steep bank to the right, rammed the throttles and propeller controls open to full power, barely avoiding the hill. But it was close, much too close.

It took me quite a few minutes to breathe easily after such a close call. I went back to the rear of the plane, where the men were being jostled roughly. They weren't sleeping anymore. They were reading magazines and looking generally unhappy.

I glanced at my watch. We had been in the air for almost an hour and fifteen minutes. I figured that in another twenty minutes or so we would be within sight of Bena Bena. The Japanese hadn't molested us yet, and from the looks of the weather ahead, there was little probability that they would be able to. The Zeros needed visual sightings to effectively bomb and strafe at Bena Bena. But I knew that if the weather got worse, we might not be able to find Bena Bena either.

The copilot came back into the cabin. He looked worried. He sat down beside me. "Major, you know how poor the maps of this country are. We've been trying to navigate at this low altitude, but since the map is so vague, we haven't the slightest idea where we are. You've flown over this part of New Guinea more. Would you come back to the cockpit and see if you can get us oriented?"

"I'll do better than that," I assured him. "I'll ask Gil Timms to take a look and see if he can spot something familiar. He's spent fifteen years in this country."

"The weather's getting better. Looks clear a few miles ahead. Soon as we get out of this scattered low stuff we should have it made."

"Yeah," I muttered, "so should the Japs."

I went across the aisle to Timms. He was sitting sideways on the seat, looking out the window. "Gil, you're needed in the cockpit. We're lost. Maybe you can give them a hand."

"Be glad to," he said. I followed him to the cockpit, where he stood between the two pilots. We sailed out from under the low clouds, almost in the clear. Peering over Timms's shoulder, I saw something that made my heart fairly leap. Several miles to our right, there was a large formation of Japanese bombers with an escort of Zeros flying parallel to our course. I touched the pilot on the shoulder.

He eased the C-47 down until we were hedgehopping the trees again. "I'll stay here as long as I can," the pilot said. Looking at Timms, he asked, "You got any idea where we are?"

Timms squinted through the windshield, moving his head from side to side. Still looking over his shoulder, I saw what I thought was the thin line of the northern New Guinea coast. At that moment I knew we had gone too far, but I didn't get a chance to tell the pilot. Timms pointed dead ahead and shouted, "You're damn right I know where we are! You see that point jutting way out in the distance?"

The pilot nodded.

"That's the Jap base at Madang!" Timms shouted. "Turn around. Get out of here. If they spot us we're dead!"

The young pilot didn't hesitate. Kicking the C-47 over on its side, he made a sharp turn to the left. The left wing tip seemed to be raking the treetops. The force of the sudden turn made my jaws sag. My body felt like dead weight as it pushed against my knees, forcing me to the floor. When the turn was completed I felt normal again. I was glad I had asked Timms to come with us — his knowledge of the country had just saved our lives.

At least now we knew where we were. The pilot drew a line on his map and measured the distance back to Bena Bena. It was forty miles, which would take about twenty minutes.

At that time, most of the maps of New Guinea — especially those that covered large areas — were plotted by hearsay. Occasionally, a lone bushman would return to civilization from a prospecting expedition with information about a river bed, or a pilot might run across an unknown mountain range or village. Rough estimates of the river's direction or the range's location and height were used to plot maps. As a result, our maps were incomplete and inaccurate.

During the early part of my tour in New Guinea, it was often necessary to have a bushman on each mission to navigate; he would help locate the outposts in need of supplies and ammunition.

The Bena Bena airstrip finally came into sight. Located on a high plateau at an elevation of more than four thousand feet, the "runway" was about thirty-three hundred feet long with a five percent grade. It was a beautiful sight, lying in the lush green of the countryside, but to the pilot making his approach, it could be treacherous and deadly. During the landing I stood between the two pilots, watching them direct the plane onto the small strip. One miscalculation on the final approach could send us crashing into the side of the plateau or, if we overshot, tumbling down the other side. The lieutenant, an excellent pilot, set the plane down smoothly, using scarcely half of the landing area.

We had hardly hit the ground when hundreds of black natives scrambled toward the airplane from every direction. I wasn't frightened since I had been to Bena Bena before, but some of the other men appeared anxious.

The natives were of all shapes and sizes, some clothed in old GI clothing and others wearing lap-laps. The majority, however, wore only leaves to cover their genitals and the children were, without exception, stark naked. Their features were broad and feral; their bodies well-built and strong-looking. I wondered how they were able to maintain such muscle on the meager food supplies they gleaned from the land.

Bena Bena was on the fringe of headhunter territory and there was every reason to believe that these natives had, not too long ago, been guilty of eating human flesh. Although the Aussies had weaned them of the habit, I wondered if they wouldn't resort to cannibalism if they were starving.

Nonetheless, we would be dependent on these natives to guide us safely into and out of headhunter territory. We would have to select guides and porters, and procure natives who had been trained by the Aussies to act as protectors and interpreters. Even though Gil Timms was thoroughly proficient in Pidgin English, there would be times when Pidgin would fail and interpreters would have to resort to the native tongue, not a word of which any of us understood.

As we unloaded our gear, the natives gathered around us and studied us and our possessions. They jabbered back and forth, pointing to us and the equipment. Several native men touched my arm and made signs which we interpreted as an offer to carry our baggage and equipment. It wasn't until Sgt. Jack Elston appeared that I was able to learn how we would procure natives to assist us.

Elston was a member of the Australian and New Guinea Administrative Unit (ANGAU), an organization charged with the administration of the Australian-mandated Territory of New

Guinea. A man of about fifty, he was as agile as a man half his age. The way he was able to make the natives listen and understand him is something I will never forget. His tongue was as sharp as any whip, and as painful.

"You've got to watch these lazy natives all the time or they'll crawl under a bush and go to sleep," Elston explained. "And you have to keep them from being too inquisitive. Oh, they're honest, all right, but what is downright thievery to us means something else to them." He turned away for a moment and reproached a native. I noticed that his Australian accent carried over to Pidgin English.

Elston walked over to our party and Timms introduced us. Elston said that they had received word that we were coming and that he was anxious to join the expedition, since he had never been in uncontrolled territory. Although Timms was technically a volunteer, he had responded to my request to join us. I was amazed that Elston would volunteer for such a trip without being asked, but he was an adventurous man, the kind that would be an asset on our mission. I didn't see how we could possibly leave him behind and I told him so. Elston was visibly pleased. We all knew that he was probably the only one in the party who could properly communicate with the natives. He explained that he would supply the native carriers and guides.

After we had unloaded our supplies, the pilot said he would like to take off immediately so he could get back to Port Moresby before the weather reached the mountains. Apparently, he wasn't as worried about the Japanese Zeros as he was about the clouds. The bombers, transports, and their fighter escorts would be on their way to bomb the Japanese targets at Lae, Salamaua, Madang, and several other locations by then. In all probability, most of the Japanese fighter planes would be concentrating on the American forces there. The lone transport would be in less danger returning to Port Moresby than it had been in coming to Bena Bena.

"Have a good trip back," I said, "and tell the boss to have a plane back here for us one week from today."

"It'll be here, Major," he said. "I'll set the flight up."

The pilots got aboard. Elston chased the natives away from the spinning propellers and the airplane taxied to takeoff position. I watched it lumber along until the wheels left the ground. I believe a small part of me left the ground with it.

Maybe we would get back in a week, maybe we wouldn't, but it was something to strive for. Not having been on an expedition like this before, I had no idea how far men could travel in a day, or how long it would take us to complete our investigation once we found the crash site. I watched our passport to civilization make a right turn and head back for Moresby. My pulse quickened a little as I realized that I was now a bushman. I wondered whether we'd be there to greet the crew when the wheels of the transport touched this runway again.

Elston and Timms called us together for a hurried conference. We decided we should make our final plans at Sigoiya, the local ANGAU headquarters. I had imagined it would be located near the airfield, but one hour and three miles later, I realized that this was just a warm-up for the journey ahead.

At Sigoiya we met Capt. John S. Hall. Timms and Elston immediately started making plans with him. The rest of us stayed in the background and remained quiet. I figured it would be better to leave the logistics to these three Aussies, since they were familiar with the natives, their habits and customs. There was no question that the natives would be reluctant to go into uncontrolled territory, where they too would be in danger. Elston would know how to handle them, to convince them to come along.

After a conference with Captain Hall and a native who appeared to be in charge of the police boys, we were assigned ten of the best police boys available. They were well-trained and disciplined, well-built and loyal. These natives were trained to supervise native activity, to go into the jungle, and — if necessary — to capture natives who violated ANGAU control rules. In addition, they often acted as guides for Australian patrols assigned to perform reconnaissance in Japanese-held territory.

Jack Elston also suggested that we take along 150 natives to carry our equipment. He examined our supplies and decided that we should take along more food. He supplied us with cheese and Australian canned beef and some trading supplies, including more salt. I didn't think we needed more than 80 men to help us, but Elston thought otherwise.

"Some of the natives will abandon the party when you enter uncontrolled territory," he said. "Others will leave when the going gets a little rougher, and if you run into trouble with the headhunters, you may be lucky if you have ten natives left to help you. Take what I've offered you, Major. You won't be sorry.

"One thing you need to remember about the natives is this," Elston added. "The normal load for a boy is forty pounds. With forty pounds he can walk indefinitely, or at least all day, provided you watch him closely. Some of the natives are cagey. They'll pick a bundle that is bulky but light and they'll strain as they lift it as if it weighs a ton. In reality the damn thing may weigh only twenty pounds. They can fool you with that trick unless you're onto them, but they can't fool Gil and me."

After Elston and Timms supervised the distribution of the loads, the bushmen set about wrapping their loads with ropes made from kunai grass — which they called gunda strips — to keep the parcels from breaking loose. If a package was too cumbersome or too heavy for one native to carry, they wrapped it around an eight-foot-long bamboo pole, making it a comfortable load for two natives walking in tandem along narrow paths.

John McGovern had appointed himself official photographer of our trip and was busy taking pictures of the preparations. Elston had a hard time keeping the natives' attention whenever McGovern had the camera pointed at them. Seeing the camera aimed his way, a native would turn, adopt the Napoleonic stance and smile, showing his large white teeth.

While the natives bound their parcels, Brady, Lock, and Reed watched them with great curiosity. Weaving in and out among the blacks, they tested their meager Pidgin English. They weren't doing so well and received the same answer from each native. In good old American slang, the natives replied, "Me no savvy."

Brady, tired of trying to communicate, picked one of the police boys to come forward and translate some orders from the *Manual of Arms*. The young policeman stood with his head erect, body straight, and huge feet splayed at a forty-five degree angle like a couple of loose boards lying on the ground. Brady gave an order and the native stared blankly, trying to comprehend him. Once he figured out what Brady was trying to say, the police boy barked the command in his native tongue, mimicking Brady's mannerisms and gestures.

Brady selected a rifle from Elston and stood in front of the native group, barking out orders in a hybrid of Pidgin and King's English. A couple of other police boys joined the contest and eventually all ten were there, trying to outdo each other as Brady commanded them. The porters left their work to watch. I could tell by their broad smiles that they were enjoying the spectacle. While this was taking place, Timms, Elston, and I sat cross-legged on the ground, hashing out some last-minute details, until the mess boy called us to dinner.

During the course of the meal, ANGAU officials offered their advice on surviving in the bush. Many of them had been bushmen before the war began, and there were few secrets of this lifestyle that they did not know. In fact, they made traveling in the bush sound extremely easy.

We joked and laughed and called each other by our first names, even though we hadn't known each other very long. A group of men with little in common had been suddenly thrown together. My men were airmen and Elston's were foot soldiers; my group was American and Elston's was Australian. Yet, there was never a gap in our conversation, there were no obstacles in our admiration for one another, no jealousies. Not even the American Army and Navy could get along as well as we were faring.

After dinner we discussed the expedition and smoked in the darkness. There were strange sounds in the night. They were probably just roaming wild pigs and wallabies or the wind whistling through the trees and brush. But there were other sounds, too. I could hear twigs cracking and I thought I even heard voices. I asked Elston about the cracking sounds but he said not to worry — they're just the sounds of Japanese patrols up to no good in the distance.

"How distant?" I asked.

"Oh, about three miles," he replied. I almost swallowed the cigarette I had just put in my mouth. "They come around this way sometimes, but they don't bother us much."

Elston didn't say much about the Japanese, but it was plain that there had been skirmishes at Sigoiya. I preferred not to mention it or even think about it, since I knew it would only keep me awake. The more I thought about it, the more voices I heard in the darkness.

At nine o'clock Elston suggested we turn in. Tomorrow would be a long day. He explained that the first day out is always the hardest. Muscles are not attuned to walking in rough terrain and feet tire easily. I was not in a position to question him.

Captain Hall put us up for the night in his mombo shack, a hut made of poles resembling bamboo and covered with thatch. We were on the crest of the mountain at an elevation of seven thousand feet. After the sun went down it became rather chilly, but it was nothing like the chill which crept into my body when I lay down to sleep. I was sure I would freeze to death before morning came, despite the fact that I was protected by a sleeping bag and three GI blankets.

When I finally fell asleep, I dreamt of Japanese patrols.

VI
KOREFEGO

"Time to snap out of it, Yanks!" Elston barked.

Rousing from my sleeping bag into the cold air the next morning brought back childhood memories of getting out of bed on cold mornings before my parents had built a fire in the coal stove that warmed our house. Many's the time I sat at the breakfast table listening to the coffee pot bubbling, waiting for a warm drink to take the chill from my body.

After I had been out of my sleeping bag for ten or fifteen minutes, a black boy came in with some tea, which I drank enthusiastically. As far as the Aussies were concerned, the war stopped during tea time. In the beginning I had scoffed at the custom, but on that first chilly morning, I thought it was one of the best traditions I had ever encountered.

At dawn I left the hut and stood outside, where the natives were hopping about the liveliest I had seen them move, building a fire. The sun was still below the hilltops, but there were gray streaks of light across the horizon. The streaks widened with each passing second, emphasizing the flat strips of thin clouds that drifted in the sky. The mountaintops were clear, devoid of the billowy cumulus clouds that would build up later in the day.

Having prepared for the trek the day before, we had little to do except eat breakfast and begin the long walk. One by one the other men ejected themselves from their sleeping bags and stumbled into the dining room, where two long wooden tables were set. Although the dishes and silverware were crude and bent, the tables were draped with white sheets, which served as tablecloths. Two native boys presented the meal with all the dignity of waiters in a formal restaurant.

To my utter amazement and chagrin, the waiters served a breakfast that consisted of toasted pork and bean sandwiches. It was the first time I had been served beans for breakfast. About the only satisfaction we received from the dehydrated eggs the Army served us was the fact that we were accustomed to eating eggs for breakfast and, dehydrated or not, they were within the confines of custom.

After a hurried breakfast, which was quite good regardless of custom, we hustled the police boys and porters together, said goodbye to the men at Sigoiya, and strung out in single file along the path that had led us to the mountaintop the day before. Elston took the lead, followed closely by the number one police boy, whose job it was to pick the trail and warn us of impending dangers from animals, the craggy terrain, headhunters, or the Japanese. Elston set the pace.

Interspersed along the long line of native porters were the other police boys, whose principal duty was to keep the carriers in line and prevent them from escaping into the bush with our rations and supplies. The last police boy brought up the rear with Timms and me. Brady and Lock were together up near the head of the line, while McGovern and Reed walked near the center of the line.

Our safari extended for almost half a mile, each man carefully picking his way over the jagged rocks and slippery trail. We all knew the first day would be the slowest, because few of us were foot soldiers. We were unaccustomed to the physical rigors of this kind of duty.

The high altitude had an almost immediate effect on us. The thin air at seven thousand feet caused shortness of breath. It took us more than an hour to cover the three miles of precipitous downgrade before we reached Bena Bena, where we had landed the day before. Although the going was rough, I knew that I hadn't seen the worst of it.

At Bena Bena we stopped for our first rest. The natives shed their packs and tied a few strands of kunai grass where the bundles appeared to be coming loose. At the station house at Bena Bena we procured more salt and shells for trading purposes. *Giri-giri* shells are small seashells measuring three-quarters to one inch long and about a half inch wide. They are roughly the shape of a lima bean and have a smooth, glossy, mother-of-pearl-like quality. The natives usually strung the shells together to make jewelry, headdresses, and wrist and arm bands, using the whole shell or just the large back center portion. When the shell was sanded until only the center back portion remained, it was referred to as a "cat's eye."

The natives also used *kinya* (gold lip) and *cuma-cuma* shells as currency. A native's wealth was judged not only by the number of pigs he owned, but also by the number of *kinya* and *cuma-cuma* shells he could call his own. The average pay for a native was one *kinya* or three *cuma-cuma* shells for three months of work. The *kinya* is a flat shell about the size of a small frying pan. The natives cut the shell into various shapes and sizes and wore it as a headdress or necklace. A native with three *kinya* shells was considered to be wealthy.

The use of salt as an item of trade may seem strange to people to whom salt is readily available, but for the natives in these remote jungle highlands, it was as precious as gold. There was no salt in the interior and there was no salt water to evaporate into salt crystals. The only salt these natives saw or tasted was transported from the coast.

After less than half an hour at Bena Bena, Elston yelled loudly, "All right, on your feet. Let's go!"

Reluctantly I got up, leaned against a small tree, and mentally swore at Elston. I was already tired and sore from the first three miles. Anyone who knew Elston knew that he did everything with enthusiasm and vigor. I suppose that was what made me feel so anxious about this mission. I feared Elston might push us so hard that some of us would say to hell with the whole thing and turn back. As I stumbled down the trail, looking clumsy compared to the sure-footed native ahead of me, I knew that I would have to dispel my negative thoughts and continue on at any cost. But it was one thing to think this and quite another to carry it out. As the chief of the party, my job was definitely cut out for me. I had to continue whether or not the others did. Backing out was not a choice.

Each of us had two natives to run errands or fill our canteens with water. My "number one boy" was a sturdy eighteen-year-old native, who was taller and much stronger than I. He carried my canteen and revolver. Carrying the pistol seemed to give him prestige among the other natives, especially since I was the boss man. My "number two boy" was a youngster of about eight who was as cute and playful as any child I had ever seen. This lad carried my camera and was my principal errand boy. As was the custom, he walked in front of me, his oversize feet as nimble as those of the grown natives. The number one boy trailed along behind, never more than a few feet away, ready to hand me my gun in case I needed it quickly.

I saw Elston coming down the line to where Timms and I were slouching along. He was carrying a kunda cane. A casualty already, I thought.

He shoved the cane at me. "This is for you, Ed," he said, smiling broadly. "I thought you might need it."

"For me?" I retorted. "Are you kidding? I'm still a young man, Jack. You'd better use it yourself."

"I've got one," he said. "Ed, it might come in handy later on." The smile had left Elston's face. Reluctantly I took the cane and thanked him.

Elston raised his hand, yelled something in Pidgin English, and the party stopped. The natives threw their packs to the ground and flopped down beside them.

Although I was already tired, I said to Elston, "Don't you think we'd better move on? We have a lot of territory to cover today."

He looked at me carefully. "You'll be ready for a rest sooner than you think, Ed. We've only started. Look back and you can still see Bena Bena. We haven't gone any distance yet."

I looked back. Elston was right. We had barely started. I thought about the long miles, the treacherous cliffs and mountains and headhunting natives still ahead of us, and lay back on the ground. Pulling my pith helmet over my eyes I said, "You're the boss, Jack."

"I believe you Americans call that 'delegation of authority,' don't you?"

"I suppose you'd call it that," I answered. Suddenly, I was very sleepy. Even though the air was crisp at our high altitude, I was sweating profusely through my shirt. "Yeah, Jack, they call it 'delegating authority.' Wake me up when it's time to go, will you?"

"Sure, Ed," he answered, clomping off toward the head of the line.

I don't know how long we remained there, but I slept the entire time. As I awoke, I heard Elston's command in Pidgin English. We were about to walk again. Groggily I sat up and blinked my eyes at what I saw. Several "Marys," our term for native women, had appeared and were jabbering with the men. They wore no clothing above the waist, exposing their pendulous breasts. Below the waist they wore short skirts of leaves. Small children cavorted nearby, chasing each other in a game. One of them darted between the legs of a porter who was adjusting his pack on his broad back. Both child and native went down, tearing the pack loose and breaking it open. Salt spilled out, and the children eagerly dug their hands into the small, soft, white mound. They stuffed the salt into their mouths, smacking their lips as though they were eating ice cream. The women also dipped into the salt and ate it, breaking into pleasant grins as they did so. Although we had lost some valuable trading goods, I didn't consider it a total waste, since the natives had received a great deal of pleasure from the accident.

I helped the porter stop the trickle of salt. He used a piece of vine to patch up the tear and slung the pack over his shoulders again, much to the chagrin of the native women, who were holding out their hands for more salt. What kept them from vomiting the salt they had already consumed I cannot say. But if I had eaten as much raw salt I would have gone into a fit of vomiting.

By the time Elston yelled out his second command to walk again, we were ready. The native women moved aside and called out a few more words to the porters as we walked past them. They were still waving when we rounded a bend in the trail.

The presence of women in the jungle was a good sign because women did not accompany the men into combat. If no women had been seen in villages as we passed them, we might have been in danger.

For the next few hours the trail was fairly smooth. The natives from the nearby village had obviously traveled it often. The loose formation of porters began singing in a steady, monotonous tone. They usually sang that way in the mornings, before too much of their energy had been sapped.

We reached the bottom of a valley and stopped beside a small, clear stream. There are hundreds of these little streams in the mountains of New Guinea; they are crystal-clear and very cold. Spanning the stream was a little wooden bridge, built by the Aussies as a show of goodwill to the natives and as a convenience for their own patrols, who were continuously going after the Japanese. Still in controlled territory, we enjoyed little conveniences like the bridge, but I knew it wouldn't always be this way.

After crossing the bridge, we started up a long grade. Halfway up the slope my pace began to slacken. Stopping, I pulled out a cigarette, took a couple of long puffs, and tossed it away.

"Ed, you want to rest awhile?" Timms asked.

"I think I'd better if I intend to stay alive," I answered, flopping down on the side of the knoll. But I got up almost immediately, afraid that if I stopped for long I might never get up again. "No, Gil, let's go on. If I sit down here I'll never get started again."

My number one boy's face betrayed a look of disgust which gave me an extra spurt of energy. The last thing I wanted was to lose face with the natives; after seeing his expression, I wouldn't have rested on that hillside for anything. I knew I might have to depend upon him in a pinch. If he lost all respect for me, I might as well not have him along.

Our procession was picking its way along a trail which wound around the saddle of two small ridges when I heard shouts. They echoed over and over, bouncing from one ridge to the other. I broke out in a cold sweat. Could it be that the hostiles were after us already? Foreign sounds of any kind in this country sent shivers up one's spine. But we were still in controlled territory; there shouldn't be a disturbance here. The Aussies had done a magnificent job of bringing the natives under their control. I turned to the nearest police boy and asked, "*Women?*" meaning, "What is it?"

"*Wandela Masta,*" he replied.

Elston came running back to my position. "What would another white man be doing here, Jack?" I asked.

"I don't know. There are still Australian prospectors here. Could be one of them."

Turning to my number one boy, I reached for my .45 pistol. Elston touched my arm. "You won't be needing that, Ed. Take a look." As the white man approached, I recognized him as Lee Mills, an Australian employed by the United States Armed Forces in the Far East. I had been introduced to him at Sigoiya. A civil engineer by trade, Mills was mapping this area for the United States Army.

"Lee, what in blazes are you doing out here alone?" I asked, surprised that he would wander around unaccompanied, even though he had spent years in New Guinea.

"It's nothing, Yank," he answered good-naturedly. "I do it all the time. I work better that way."

"One of these days you'll lose your head to a Jap patrol," Elston kidded him, "or a bad native."

"I'll chance it. I'd like to join your party, Major. The land you're headed into has never been surveyed. It's a wonderful opportunity."

"We'd like to have you, Lee," I said, "but where's your equipment?"

Mills looked at me and laughed loudly. "Oh, my equipment! Well, I suppose as a surveyor I'm not quite as modern as one might think. I have no equipment except these."

He pulled out a pencil, a small notebook, and some *giri-giri* shells. Around his neck was a small compass.

"You see, I can get my course fairly accurate with this," he explained, fingering the instrument strung around his neck. "I have to estimate the elevations, but they'll be fairly accurate. For the distance, I have another method: these *giri-giri* shells." He held them out for us to see. "Each time I count one hundred paces I shift one shell from my right pocket to my left. That way I can figure distances fairly accurately."

"Well, I'll be damned!" I said. "What would become of this world if it weren't for all you clever Aussies?"

"Well, there are no other methods available to us. Most of the surveys of New Guinea have used guesswork. My methods are guesswork, too, but for the most part, they're fairly accurate. At least accurate enough to fight a war."

"Since you put it that way, Lee, what can I say? That's what we're out here for . . . to fight a war. Grab a place in line. You just got yourself a slot on this safari."

"I'll make a map if you'd like," Mills said.

"You'd better. We have to get out of this place after we've gotten in!"

The rest of the party had moved ahead while we stood and talked briefly. They were out of sight by the time we hit the trail again.

Walking at a steady pace, Mills counted paces to himself, occasionally shifting a *giri-giri* shell to his left pocket.

"You can do that while you're talking?" I asked.

"There's nothing difficult about it. One gets used to it. Like a wireless operator who can send a message by the dot-dash system and talk with someone at the same time." Mills was right. I had seen this back in my old outfit in the States. One of our sergeants could tap out a message on the sending bug while reading a newspaper or talking.

Each time the path took a turn, no matter how slight, Mills would turn around, take his bearing, then jot the figures down in his notebook. This was Lee Mills: well-educated, intelligent, quiet, and as steady as the raised arm of the Statue of Liberty.

About a mile ahead of us was the Bena Bena River. I knew the rest of the party would wait for us there.

At the river each person in the party had to wait his turn to cross the swinging bridge. The Aussies had constructed it with planks laid end to end, resting on crosspieces of two-by-fours. The two-by-fours rested on steel cables, which were anchored at both ends of the bridge. Two cables, strung across at shoulder height about an arm's span apart, were used for balance when the bridge swayed from side to side. I wondered why the Japanese hadn't destroyed the bridge, but I realized that it was as convenient for them as it was for the Aussies. The Japanese wouldn't destroy it unless such action was absolutely necessary.

I looked down at the jagged rocks sticking up from the swiftly moving stream thirty feet below. One slip of the foot, one lost handhold, and I could plummet to my death. If the fall didn't kill me, the swift water would either drown me or batter me against the rocks. The natives walked across easily, their black bodies swaying in rhythm with the bridge. The Aussies were a bit clumsier and occasionally lunged to grab the cables. But we Americans were the worst of all. We clung to the cables and walked slowly and gingerly. Only three people could cross the bridge at a time, so I crossed with my two native boys. Again I saw my number one boy stare disgustedly at me, showing his displeasure at my awkwardness.

A few miles later we stopped for lunch. We had been walking on hilly paths for almost six hours. I was beginning to feel the strain. Going downhill we had to grasp bushes for support or we would slide and fall on the slippery mud. Going uphill, we grasped the bushes to pull ourselves along and to keep from sliding backwards. It had been years since I had done anything that even resembled hiking. Neither my stomach muscles, nor my feet and legs, were up to it.

As the cooks made sandwiches and tea, I lay down and tried to rest. It gave me a tremendously weak feeling to know that we had come such a short way and that we still faced so much territory. Although my body was ready to quit, I could not tolerate the thought of failure. Here I was, an American airman — well trained and, for all practical purposes, in excellent physical condition — feeling unable to live up to the task I had been assigned.

Like other American soldiers, I was considered fit for the duty in New Guinea. Yet the natives who accompanied us — who had received no formal training whatsoever — made us look like undisciplined boys. I wished that we "sophisticated" Americans could be as physically capable as these "simple" natives.

I pulled out a cigarette, lit it, and handed it to a porter who readily accepted it. I had suddenly decided to give up smoking. But, of course, my resolution didn't last. Within minutes, I had pulled out another cigarette and lit it for myself.

Rolling over on my elbow, I glanced up at Mills and asked, "How far have we come?"

"About six miles," he answered nonchalantly.

"Six miles? Good Lord, Lee, I've never walked this far at one time in my life! Six miles!"

"You've only begun."

"Don't remind me. Say, what about all the movies I've seen where the native porters make litters out of poles and vines and carry their white master?"

"That's a figment of the imagination of some Hollywood producer, Major. I never heard of it out here. Not in New Guinea."

"Maybe we should start a new fad."

"Fad?"

"Sure. Let's teach the natives how to make the litters, then explain to them that they're behind the times, that they need to take better care of their white masters."

"These natives have no white masters. Just because they're accompanying us on this trek is no assurance they'll stay or even do as we tell them to. The police boys . . . they're different. They're well trained and loyal and will help us keep the safari together, even in the face of danger from the cannibals."

"They wouldn't go for carrying us on litters, eh?"

"Forty pounds apiece is about their limit. Put another ounce on them and they'll balk like llamas. They'll simply quit and go back to their villages.

"But it's a nice try, Major," Mills said, grinning at me and rolling a cigarette in a piece of brown paper.

I took an extra pack of cigarettes from my shirt pocket and handed it to him. The pack was crumpled but the cigarettes inside were still good. He stuffed the brown paper and sack of tobacco back in his shirt pocket and buttoned the flap. Then he removed his hat and mopped his brow with his shirt sleeve. "Thanks, Major. One thing you Yanks have is a good cigarette."

"Yeah, they've been good to me. Look at me now, a perfect specimen of good health."

"Have one," Mills suggested, extending the open pack.

"Thanks," I said, "Don't mind if I do."

The cook brought us sandwiches made from canned Australian meat, which we called bully beef, and a tin cup of tea. I was so hungry I finished mine quickly and watched Mills munching away at his. "One thing you've got to remember out here, Major, is to take it easy," he said. "Do everything slow . . . like eating. It'll stay with you longer than if you cram it down quickly."

I hadn't said three words to the other Americans in the group all morning. Since we were so spread out along the column, there was little sense in yelling back and forth, expending what little energy we had left. At lunchtime, I was finally able to speak with them. Lock, Brady, and the others came and flopped down on the ground beside me. We chatted for a few minutes, then Brady and Lock got up and started looking for something. Gil Timms tossed an empty cigarette package to them. Apparently, it was what they wanted. Lock walked back to us, and Brady stuck the empty package on the limb of a low bush. Lock loosened his holster and took out his .45 pistol.

"What're you going to do?" I asked.

"I'm going to hit that paper," Lock answered, checking the slide and clip of his gun.

"From that distance? With a .45?"

Brady cut in. "The guy's crazy as a loon. Just a minute ago, he told me how good he was . . . it would take a pretty good shot."

"You're dreaming, Lock. Maybe with a rifle you could do it," I said skeptically.

"Sometime I'll show you all the cups and medals I've won with a rifle," Lock said.

"Yeah," Brady said. "With a rifle. But you're holding a pistol."

"Pistol, schmistel, who cares? It's a gun, isn't it?" Lock flipped back the hammer and leveled the barrel of the .45 at the empty cigarette package. His hand was perfectly motionless.

Watching Lock sitting poised to shoot was something I'll never forget. It was almost as if his heart had stopped beating so it would not disturb his aim. Then there was a faint movement as the second knuckle on the forefinger of his right hand moved, taking up the last remaining slack on the trigger. The finger tensed ever so slightly and pressed gently without disturbing the rest of his hand.

Even before I was conscious of the blast of the cartridge, I saw a neat, blue hole appear in the center of the cigarette pack. The paper swayed gently for an instant, then steadied again. Aside from the kick of the explosion, Lock's gun hadn't moved. It was back in its original position and Lock was sighting along the top of the barrel. There was another explosion and the gun bucked. Twice more he fired and the cigarette package twitched slightly as the bullets ripped through. After the fourth shot I got up and ran to the paper and grabbed it. There were four holes, spaced closely enough together that a half dollar would cover them. I tossed the paper to Mills.

"How's that for shooting, Lee?" I asked, embarrassed by having played the part of the skeptic.

Mills looked at Lock and extended the bullet-riddled paper to him. "I'd like to keep this, Captain, if you don't mind. My friends back at Sigoiya will find it hard to believe."

"Imagine what he could do to a group of men with that gun," Brady said.

"I've never shot at a man. I hope I never have to," Lock responded. "Bomb them, yes. But look a man in the face and shoot him with a gun . . . I don't think I could."

We were resting — sprawled out on the ground — and thinking about Lock's words, when McGovern suddenly yelled, "Hey, take a look at this!"

We leapt up, not sure what to expect. My first thought was that there was a disturbance among the natives. But McGovern had called attention to something he was holding in his hand.

"What's up?" I asked.

"Nothing's up. I've just invented a new kind of sandwich!"

He was holding what we would later refer to as the "biscuit sandwich." It consisted of a biscuit between two pieces of cheese.

"Use the gun on him, Lock," I said.

"He's not worth the bullet, Lock," Reed added. "Let's give him to the cannibals instead."

"Okay," McGovern replied. "But you guys were getting morbid. Someone had to break it up." McGovern wasn't so dumb. After his remark, we realized that he had a store of common sense in that balding gray head.

Soon we were on our way again. Though the rest and the lunch were refreshing, we needed to make as much progress this day as possible. I felt as though I was walking knee-deep in butter. After a few minutes, however, my legs became more limber and the walk was more bearable.

Contrary to the advice of Gil Timms, I rolled up my sleeves as the day grew warmer. My arms were becoming sunburned but I wasn't aware of it. But when we reached an area covered with ten-foot-high kunai grass, I became acutely aware of my trouble. The razor-sharp blades sent searing pain through my arms each time I brushed up against them. It was impossible to avoid the grass, since our path went directly through the field of kunai grass. I had to clear a path with my cane, which slowed me down.

Within an hour the pain had become unbearable; I was cut and bleeding from knuckles to elbow. For the rest of the afternoon, the going was plain drudgery. The Japanese air raids on Port Moresby seemed like child's play compared with this torture. Good old Beam, I thought, sitting back there at our base as smug as sin.

Late in the afternoon we came to the village of Korefego. The aerial maps I was accustomed to didn't show the names of villages. The maps used by American aviators simply had a little round circle labeled with the generic term "village." There were several of those circles on our charts; none of them was named.

As we approached Korefego the natives came out in force to meet us, lining the path like a crowd of New Yorkers on St. Patrick's Day. Although their faces beamed smiles of welcome, I didn't feel comfortable standing among them — these natives practically lived in the backyard of headhunters. Apparently, neither many white visitors nor even many natives from other villages came to see them, so this was quite a special occasion.

I was feeling so bad by this time, however, that I cared little about the friendly natives. My arms burned like fire. Two sturdy natives approached me. Suddenly, one of them grabbed my right arm and the other the left. I cast a questioning glance at Timms, but all I received in return was a smile.

"What's this all about?" I asked loudly, wanting to pull away from the iron grasp of these two burly blacks. The natives smiled at me and stared at my arms. I gave them a quick smile in return as a sort of appeasement — I didn't know what to expect from them — and wondered what was going to happen next. I was convinced they were salivating as they rubbed the hair on my arms. The touch of their rough, scaly hands made the cuts burn even more fiercely, and I winced at the pain.

"Gil, are you sure these natives are friendly?" I asked. "They seem to be sizing me up for soup."

Timms chuckled and said, "You see, Ed, these natives have no hair on their arms or legs."

I looked at the men holding onto me. Sure enough, there was only light fuzz on their extremities.

"Seeing anyone with as much hair on his arms as you have is quite a novelty to them."

"Let them go rub someone else's arms. It hurts like hell."

"These are affectionate people, Ed. They mean no harm. It's just their way of doing things."

"Let them be affectionate with someone else, Gil. I've had enough."

"I guess you didn't see the natives greeting each other," Timms said.

"I could care less," I answered, pulling myself away from the two men as firmly as I could without offending them.

"You would," Elston interrupted, "if they greeted you."

"The common greeting for natives in these parts is to embrace you and rub your genitalia," Timms explained.

"What? Rub my what?"

"You heard what I said."

"Damn right I heard what you said, Jack, but I don't believe it. I'd clobber the first one that laid a . . ."

"See those natives coming up the hill now?" Timms asked. "Watch them. If they know any of the carriers in our group, they'll exchange greetings in the usual way."

"I'd better watch this myself," Brady interjected. "Might learn something."

The other men snickered at Brady, the youngest in the group. "Yeah, he-man, maybe you will," Lock said. "But don't try to practice these native customs anywhere else!"

I watched as the group of natives coming up the hill approached our porters. When they were still several yards apart, some of the natives recognized each other and started running. When the first native reached one of our men, he began to gently rub his crotch and then his leg.

"What's the significance of it, Gil?" I asked.

"Can't say that I know, Ed, except that it's a native custom that's been practiced for eons."

"Have you ever been greeted like that?"

"To tell you the truth, I haven't. I was, however, on hand when the first white women arrived in these parts and got the native greeting."

"Must have been interesting."

"Very interesting."

Brady piped up, "I'm all ears."

"This was quite some time ago," Timms began, "even before the natives had grown accustomed to seeing many white men around. This woman was the wife of an ANGAU official who was coming to live here. I helped fly her in. I warned her beforehand that she would have to get used to many unusual things. I told her that she would be on her own and would have to show the natives that she had the strength of character to weather New Guinea. She told me she could handle any situation. After all, she said, she had been in government service for quite some time and wasn't about to be scared away by ignorant, primitive natives.

"The old girl was dressed in slacks, and rather tight ones at that, when she stepped from the plane. To the natives, she was just another man, except that she had long blond hair. Perhaps it was the hair that made her the center of attention. The natives swarmed around her.

"One of the local chieftains, eager to welcome this newcomer to the territory and to put himself in good with the local Australian constabulary, walked up to her mumbling in Pidgin English, beamed a huge smile, and let his hand fall to her legs, and then, to her crotch.

"She stood there for a moment wearing the most puzzled expression I have ever seen. The puzzlement turned to beet red anger and all this time the chief simply grinned, enjoying the fact that he was the first one to make contact with the newcomer — official contact, that is.

"Suddenly, the lady who said she could take care of herself did so. Up from near the ground came a right hook, a haymaker that landed squarely on the bridge of the grinning chief's nose. The grin changed to complete surprise as he stumbled backward and fell on his behind. Rubbing his chin, he looked back at the white woman, got up and scrambled away while the other natives laughed until tears ran down their cheeks."

When we finally got down to business, the native chief and Gil discussed where we would spend the night. The chief pointed to a hut built of mombo poles and kunai grass.

Our porters put our packs and bundles on the ground near the hut. Then they dispersed to visit with the locals, which gave us a chance to set up our sleeping bags and get settled. After a few minutes in the hut, I was ready to spend the night in the bush. Fleas were as thick as flies around a sugar bowl. The vermin attacked us as soon as we were under the enclosure.

I heard McGovern swear loudly and watched him squirm as

some of the fleas got inside his clothing. "There's only one answer to this," he said. "As soon as we get into the bags, we'll use the aerosol bombs and spray the hell out of them. Then we'll have to keep the sacks zipped up all night."

"We'll smother inside them," Reed complained.

Elston interrupted. "It'll get cold here tonight. I think Mac has the right idea. Take an aerosol bomb inside your sleeping bags with you, zip up the bag, and give a few good healthy squirts with the bomb. It'll kill the varmints."

"It'll kill us too," Reed protested.

"Suit yourself, mate," Timms said, walking away. "But I'm going to do as McGovern said. After a few bites you'll change your bloody mind, Reed."

The natives unpacked our things and the cooks returned to prepare supper for us. We sat outside the mombo hut, away from the fleas, amusing ourselves by watching the natives who amused themselves by watching us. Dozens of natives were standing around us, mumbling and jabbering among themselves but not bothering anyone. Then I noticed that one of the Marys seemed to have taken a shine to me. It was almost impossible to keep her out of my line of sight. I tried looking off in another direction, but she would walk in that direction until I was looking at her again. Each time she caught my eye she would grin at me, winking ever so slightly. She looked to be about seventy years old and had so many wrinkles that it was difficult to tell for sure whether she was smiling or not. She only had one tooth, and it glared at me like a rock's pinnacle every time she opened her mouth.

Elston saw me trying to avoid her gaze. "How old do you think she is, Major?"

"About seventy or eighty," I guessed.

"She's probably forty at the most. They age quickly here," he explained. "You seldom see one who has reached seventy. They age very rapidly living so close to nature. This one's already over the hill; '*Lapun pinis*,' they call it in Pidgin English. It means she can't have babies anymore."

"Thanks," I said jokingly. "I'm glad to hear that."

She walked by me again, grinned, showing her single tooth, and muttered something I couldn't understand. I was embarrassed, but the rest of the men were getting a kick out of it.

Two little boys the Australians called their monkeys approached us and McGovern handed them cigarettes. They put the cigarettes into their mouths and posed proudly as McGovern took their picture. They couldn't have been more than five or six years old but they knew what to do with a cigarette. As soon as McGovern snapped the picture an old man ran up, grabbed the cigarettes out of the boys' mouths, and began smoking one of them himself.

Natives began arriving with food to trade. They came with *kau kau* — a native sweet potato — sweet corn, sugar cane, and beans. Our police boys tried to control the crowd by arranging the natives in a circle and instructing them to wait there. The police boys then worked their way around the circle, dishing out a spoonful of salt and a couple of *giri-giri* shells to each native. In return, the natives turned all their food over to us. Apparently, they were satisfied that the police boys had given each of them a fair trade. Their faces showed their happiness.

When the police boy dropped the spoonful of salt into the open palm of a native, the recipient would carefully transfer it into a hollow bamboo shaft for storage. The natives licked the few remaining grains off their hands and smacked their lips in delight.

The local chief had organized a special sing-sing in our honor. The native songs were monotonous and high-pitched, similar to Gregorian chants, using no more than five or six notes. The singing was accompanied by a number of flutelike wooden instruments hollowed out of bamboo stalks, and drums constructed of animal skin stretched over a barrel-like casement. The music created a great deal of excitement among the natives and they danced wildly, their bodies writhing in a contorted fashion and bouncing up and down.

The cooks began to prepare some of the food we had just purchased. By the time we had finished eating, it was dark. According to Lee Mills, we had walked about twelve miles over difficult terrain that day. We were exhausted.

We crawled into our sleeping bags. Tomorrow we would be in uncontrolled territory. There would be no prominent boundary line marking the end of controlled territory, but the natives would know. Their intuition was uncanny. I knew that the second we stepped into headhunter country the faces of the natives would show it.

Before I fell asleep, I thought about how years ago — even days ago — this mission would have sounded absurd to me. I could never have imagined myself in this situation, miles from nowhere in the heart of New Guinea. If man were permitted to look into the future, I feel certain he would die on the spot from sheer fright.

The last thing I remember saying before I dropped off to sleep was that I wished Colonel Beam were here suffering with us, but no one heard me. They were all asleep. I sprayed the inside of my sleeping bag and zipped it closed.

VII

UNCONTROLLED TERRITORY

The aerosol bomb we used on the fleas did the trick. I wasn't bothered the entire night. My tossing and turning probably killed those fleas which had not been exterminated by the spray. The hard ground of the mombo hut was incredibly uncomfortable. We were much warmer than the night before, but I had a hard time getting out of my sleeping bag in the morning. My limbs and body had been stiff when I crawled into the sleeping bag, but now they felt like wood. When I finally stood up, I tried to work the stiffness and soreness out by exercising, but my body was reluctant to respond. Now I understood why the Army insisted that we exercise strenuously at least three hours a week. Until now, I had disobeyed this order, using my busy pilot's schedule as an excuse. Had I complied with the order, this trip would have been much easier for me. "When you get back, Imparato," I told myself, "you are going to start obeying that order. Let this be a lesson!"

The natives were already making breakfast and preparing the packs for the day's journey when Lock and I dragged ourselves to the little fire outside the hut. The Australians were as pleasant as ever. Brady, Reed, and McGovern sat by themselves in the darkness staring into the fire. I went over and sat down beside them and lit a cigarette. My mouth tasted cottony from not having brushed my teeth. I could also taste the effects of the aerosol bomb I had sprayed inside my sleeping bag. I blew out a huge puff of smoke and let it float around my face. I turned to Brady. "It doesn't compare to Australia, does it?"

"Compare? It shouldn't even be mentioned in the same breath, Major."

"You want to see that girl, don't you?"

"More than anything else in the world right now," he said. There was a faraway tone, a sadness, in his voice.

"You'll see her, buddy — real soon," I assured him. "I'll see that you get to Australia in style."

"I'll go any way I can get there," he said quietly. "Any way I can." He stared into the distance. The tone of his voice was incongruous with the happy chatter of the natives. I couldn't blame the boy. I knew very little about his background, his personal life, but I was quite sure he hadn't been far from home when the bugle call sounded him to arms. Brady was a country boy. It was evident in his speech, in his manner, in his walk, and in his openness.

After a hurried breakfast, we fell into line again, and Elston led us out of the village toward uncharted, and uncontrolled, territory. For the first two hours, walking was incredibly difficult. It would only get worse; we were passing into even more rugged terrain. There were no footpaths to follow. We had to pick our way along the stream beds, through thick kunai grass and marshland. My feet got wet and my socks began to crawl down into my shoes. I had to stop every few yards to pull them up again. The pain eventually left my body and numbness took over. For the next few hours, walking became a mechanical process; I concentrated on placing one foot in front of the other.

I had no feeling, no reaction to the sharp, slippery rocks or the sticky mud. I wanted to lie down and not get up, to tell the rest of the party to go on without me. Although I didn't know it at the time, the others were of the same state of mind. Even Timms, the tough Australian, was beginning to show signs of exhaustion. Thoughts of the report I had to get to General Whitehead somehow kept me going. Had it been for almost any other cause, I probably would have called for a retreat and headed back to Bena Bena and waited for the C-47 that would arrive in a few days.

Above top, *Maj. Gen. Ennis C. Whitehead, Commander, Advance Echelon, Fifth Air Force.* **Right,** *Col. Roger Beam, acting commanding officer of the 374th Troop Carrier Group.* **Above,** *Col. Ed Imparato. This picture was taken after the mission.*

We had hardly hit the ground when hundreds of natives scrambled to the airplane from every direction. **Left,** The headdresses these men are wearing are made from kunai grass, tree bark, and plant stems. The decorative shells piercing their noses are called kinya (or gold-lip). Female Papuans rarely wear kinya shells. **Below,** Some of the native men were clothed in old GI uniforms and others wore lap-laps.

This picture was taken at our forward airfield at Bena Bena, where we assembled our supplies and hired natives to serve as carriers and police boys. Left to right: Gil Timms, Ed Imparato, John "Mac" McGovern, Bill Brady, and Paul Reed.

Above, The head police boy followed Jack Elston, who led our expedition. It was the head police boy's job to pick the trail and warn us of impending dangers from animals, the craggy terrain, headhunters, or the Japanese. **Left,** The other police boys were charged with keeping the carriers in line and preventing them from escaping into the bush with our rations and supplies.

The natives were well-built and strong-looking. I wondered how they were able to maintain their incredible muscle tone on the meager food supplies they gleaned from the land.

The view of the outpost at Bena Bena as we began the first leg of our journey.

We encountered this group of typical-looking Papuan men at Bena Bena.

The tall grass in the foreground is kunai grass which can cut right through skin. Kunai grass grows ten to twelve feet high in the jungles of New Guinea. We stored our drinking water in the long, hollow bamboo poles the natives are shouldering.

Jack Elston stands at the head of the long string of carriers shortly after our departure from Bena Bena. Our safari extended for nearly half a mile.

Above, *Lewis Lock, the crack shot, with a police boy, left, and a carrier, right.* **Left,** *This is my number two boy, an eight-year-old who was killed when we were attacked by hostile natives. Each of us was assigned two natives to run errands, such as filling our canteens with water.* **Right,** *This is one of the bamboo bridges we encountered in controlled territory. Although it is crude-looking, it was safe.*

There was only one way to cross the Dunantina River: by wading. The natives carried us on their backs; it took over an hour for the entire party to cross, but we didn't lose a man.

Lewis Lock, left, and Bill Brady, right, cooling off in a stream near the village of Tunofi, in the heart of uncontrolled territory. Shortly after this picture was taken, Brady, Lock, and I were attacked.

This picture was taken about ten miles outside of Bena Bena. When a package was too heavy for one carrier, the load was hung on a bamboo pole so that the burden could be shared by two or three carriers.

The presence of women in the jungle was a good sign because women did not accompany the men into combat. If we didn't see women, we knew we were in danger. Papuan women gathered wood every day and they usually carried the burden on their heads. Some of the women have pierced their noses with a small twig.

Above, *The caps and skirts worn by these women are woven from tree bark and kunai grass and the bands around their waists and arms are made from tree bark and plant stems. Their necklaces are made of giri-giri shells. The woman on the right is also wearing a cumma-cumma shell, which is the size and shape of a lemon.* **Right,** *This native has a decomposed finger hanging from his ear. In Papua, it was common practice for family members to wear a finger or another body part of a deceased relative as a token of respect. The custom was intended to please the spirit of the departed.*

A chieftain in the village of Korefego organized this sing-sing in our honor. The natives' costumes are made from the products of the jungle: kunai grass, bamboo shoots, wild flowers, plant stems, and tree bark.

Left, This native is demonstrating a hunting bow. Poison arrows, which are very hard to manufacture, are used sparingly. Poison arrows are fitted with a loose head, which becomes detached in the wound. The foreshaft of the arrow is usually covered with a poison latex, which dissolves in the wound, usually causing a fatal infection. **Below,** These men are wearing gourds to protect their genitalia and to symbolize their manhood. The small bags they have slung over their shoulders were used to carry potatoes left over from breakfast and sugar cane. **Right,** The ceremonial headdresses worn by these men are made of kinya shells, jungle plants and flowers, and the black feathers of the cassowary bird. The decorations hanging from their armbands are snake skins; we also saw Papuan men wearing the skins of wallabies, giant rats, and pigs.

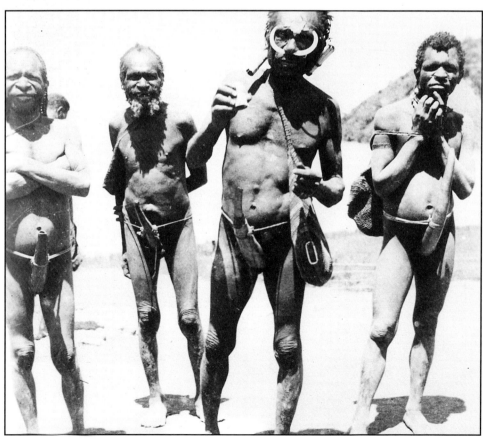

Jack Elston, surrounded by police boys and carriers, interrogates a hostage.

Lee Mills took this picture shortly before Brady was killed. Bottom row, left to right: *John "Mac" McGovern and Lewis Lock.* Top row, left to right: *Jack Elston, Bill Brady, Paul Reed, Ed Imparato, and Gil Timms.*

These natives surrendered after Brady had been injured in the skirmish at the crash site. We questioned them at length about the wreckage of the B-24 and found several natives who had witnessed the mysterious crash.

During his interrogation, this native — one of the eyewitnesses — indicated the direction of the B-24 just prior to the crash. "Straight down," he said. Jack Elston is sitting on the crate and I am to his right.

The left wing showed serious impact damage. The wing butts were scorched, which indicated that they had been destroyed on impact by the explosion or the resulting fire. Parts of the wing and aileron assemblies were missing; they were either destroyed on impact or removed from the scene by the natives.

Above top, The right vertical stabilizer, which was found almost a mile from the crash site, was virtually unscathed. There was no sign of damage from the impact of the crash or the heat and fire of the explosion. **Above,** Of the ten to twenty bombs the B-24 carried, only one remained unexploded. We found this bomb at the center of the crash site.

The natives built a small hut out of the left vertical and horizontal stabilizer. We left these parts of the tail assembly exactly as we found them, since they provided no evidence that would contribute to our investigation.

Above top, *The nature of the terrain at the crash site helped us to determine the path of the B-24 just prior to impact. Because there was no impact damage or scarring of the soil on the many hills that surrounded the crash site, we decided that the crash occurred as a result of a near-vertical descent.* **Above,** *The B-24 had four engines, but we only found the #3 engine of the downed craft at the crash site. We did find small pieces of engine parts, which indicated that the other three engines had still been intact on impact. They were probably consumed by the intense heat of the explosion and fire.*

The B-24 had been flying north toward its target at the Japanese base at Madang when it crashed. The wings separated from the fuselage on impact, moving away from the center of the explosion and escaping damage from the heat of the fire.

Above, The center section of the horizontal stabilizer showed clear evidence that metal tear forces, forces beyond the tensile strength of the metal's design capacity, were the cause of the crash. Progressive fractures, such as the ones that caused this crash, are often due to the vibration of the vertical fin over a long period of time under overload conditions, such as those frequently experienced in combat. **Left,** We sent the right horizontal stabilizer to the metallurgy lab in Brisbane, Australia, for verification of our findings.

Our final salute to the downed airmen.

As I walked, I thought about a story my fourth grade teacher had read to me. It was called *A Message to Garcia*. During the Spanish American War, President William McKinley needed to get an urgent message to Garcia, an insurgent who was fighting the Spanish in the jungles of Cuba. The President needed someone with spirit and determination to get the difficult job done. One of his staff members said he knew a fellow by the name of Rowan who could get the job done. Rowan surmounted great difficulties and hardships to deliver the President's message. Remember Rowan, I told myself again and again. He didn't let anything stop him from completing his mission.

The sun burned through the late morning clouds and it got hotter. Sweat thoroughly sopped our clothing. Swarms of tiny black flies followed us and became entangled in our stubby beards. We had to pick them out one by one and crush them. As we walked along through the tangled growth, ants and other insects clung to our clothing or crawled under it and bit us. Scratching the bug bites and smashing the insects on our skin caused huge blisters. Elston spent a great deal of time helping the Americans break open the blisters and daub them with iodine. I tried killing the flying creatures with insecticide, but to no avail.

I felt something on my leg. Pulling up my trousers, I saw a huge leech which had already buried half its body into my flesh and had sucked so much of my blood that it looked like a baby blimp. I started to reach for the thing, but Timms grabbed my arm.

"No, no, Ed. That's not the way. Do that and you'll leave half the bloody varmint under your skin."

He took out a cigarette, lit it, and touched the lighted end to the leech. Its fat tail quivered and the leech released its grip. Timms pulled it off my leg and squashed it against the ground with the toe of his boot. The leech left a dark red hole about the size of a pinhead on my leg. I took some iodine from my first aid kit and daubed it on. The iodine stung, but the pain was nothing compared to the feeling of a blood-sucking leech fattening itself on my blood.

I wondered if the headhunters were more deadly than the natural dangers we faced. At least we could protect ourselves against them. We could see them and shoot them. We had already had more than our share of hardships and we'd been out less than two days. How much worse could it get?

Just before noon we stopped along the banks of a swift river about seventy-five feet wide. Rocks connecting the river's banks formed a natural ford. We judged the depth of the water to be no more than four or five feet. The river was called the Dunantina. It was swift because its source was located in a mountain range nine thousand feet above sea level. Where we stood was about five thousand feet above sea level. The Dunantina was too wide for the natives to construct a bridge across, and since white men had no reason to cross the river, they hadn't built one either.

There was only one way to cross: by wading. Elston informed me that he didn't want any white man to attempt the crossing alone. The natives, being more sure-footed, would cross the river carrying us on their backs.

I questioned Elston's reasoning. He didn't want white men crossing the river alone because even the sure-footed natives would find it difficult. But they were supposed to carry us across, struggling with a load of dead weight while trying to maintain their balance. Yet, who was I to argue with Elston? He had spent many years in New Guinea and undoubtedly knew what he was talking about. I also realized he would not deliberately submit a native to a task that might cause injury or death. If Elston made them take too many risks, he would lose the respect of the natives and they would desert us.

Watching the natives begin to cross the roaring stream made my skin crawl. The first native entered the water and promptly lost his footing. He also lost one of our packs, which was swept downstream, out of reach. I watched it pound against one rock after another until the contents were scattered on the river's surface, swirling away. If this was any indication of what was to come, then I was ready to turn back. This mission, I began to think, was not worth our lives. The crew of the downed plane had already been killed. Why add other names to the death roster?

But the first three natives made it across, giving us all some hope. Elston was next. He picked a huge, sturdy native and straddled his broad back. The native grasped Elston's legs with his huge hands and waded into the stream. He faltered, regained his footing, and then crossed with surprising ease. The others followed safely, without losing another parcel. I was last.

My number one boy handed my gun to my number two boy and pointed to the stream. The eight-year-old walked into the water without hesitation and began making his way from rock to rock, burdened by the camera and the gun. When he was safe on the other side he turned and waved to us, a sign that we should start across.

Number one boy bent down so I could lock my legs around him in a saddle grip. I clinched my feet together tightly around his middle and he grasped my ankles. Then, clutching his shoulders as tightly as I could and turning my face to avoid the smell of his greasy hair, I braced myself for the initial impact with the water. The boy stepped into the river, stopped for a moment, readjusted me, then took an unsteady step forward. He had to stop again to maintain his balance. I remained perfectly still, lest I cause both of us to fall.

For the next few minutes he picked his way precariously through the maze of rocks. Halfway across he stopped beside a large rock to catch his breath. I could feel his huge barrel chest heaving as he stood there. Sweat poured from the pores of his oily skin, making it difficult to maintain my grasp on his bare shoulders. Relaxing my grip once to wipe my hands on my trousers, I noticed my fingertips had left an imprint on his skin.

I could see Elston squatting on the far bank, watching me closely. I thought I saw him squirm occasionally, moving his body in the same rhythm as the native who was carrying me, as if trying to guide my number one boy.

After what seemed like hours in the torrent, my number one boy lowered me gently to the ground. I sank down beside Elston. The native sprawled out on the ground with his eyes closed. I wanted to shake his hand and thank him for the job he had done, but I knew Elston would object to such familiarity. Instead, I lay there and watched the native's great black chest heave, expanding and shrinking as he regained his wind.

It took a little more than an hour for the entire party to make the crossing, but we didn't lose a man. In fact, we lost only the one pack which the first native had dropped. That was all. Watching the natives cross the Dunantina with such skill had increased my admiration for them. I was glad they were on our side, that they were there to help us.

After we had rested for half an hour, the cooks began to prepare food. The crossing had bolstered our spirits and we were all in good humor. The natives seemed to sense that we were pleased with what they had done and they went about repairing their packs, singing their same old chant which sounded more lively and rhythmic to me that day.

The trek was beginning to wear on us. Reed's and McGovern's faces looked haggard and drawn. It was sheer fortitude and determination that had carried us this far. Brady and Lock seemed to be in the best physical shape of all the Americans. It hurt my pride a little to know that they were in much better condition than I. I could not imagine what I looked like, probably something like Reed and McGovern, since I was a little older than Brady and Lock. The three Aussies seemed to take the trek in stride, as if they did this sort of thing every day. Though their faces were unshaven and their clothing dirty and sweat-soaked, their walk and actions were still as brisk as ever.

When the natives brought our lunch, we ate with real relish for the first time since the beginning of the trip. Crossing the river safely had done something to us. It had been our most formidable obstacle so far, and we had overcome it without difficulty.

During the course of lunch we discussed the terrain ahead. The mountains had an ominous look, seeming to lunge at us and say, "Try us if you dare." The peaks were high and ragged, and the altitude would soon tell on us.

Elston got up and stretched. After removing his crumpled Aussie hat and tossing it on the ground, he brushed a long lock of sandy hair out of his eyes.

"From now on every man will carry his own gun. Be sure it's loaded. Keep your native boys beside you at all times to carry extra ammunition. You've probably guessed it already, but in case you haven't, we're in uncontrolled territory now, land of the headhunters."

VIII
TUNOFI VILLAGE

Our total armament consisted of seven .45 pistols, two carbines, ten Australian .303s, and one Bren gun. Although we knew our weapons would be superior to native bows and arrows, we realized that we faced the chance of being greatly outnumbered if we were attacked.

The arrowheads the natives used were covered with sharp, needlelike barbs. Once imbedded in the flesh, the arrow could not be removed without cutting away the flesh around it. Although I hoped for the best, the stories I had heard indicated that the natives would attack if they thought we were intruding on their domain.

It's odd how a man worries about what will happen to his body after he dies. Though I knew full well that I would not feel anything should I be killed by an arrow, I was horrified by the thought that I might be carved up like an animal and eaten. I tried not to think about it, but it was hard to shake such thoughts.

The Aussies had insight into the native mind that enabled them to anticipate the actions and reactions of the natives we encountered. Our police boys had proven to be loyal and capable. American eyes could never look into the bush and see what they saw; American ears could never hear the footsteps they heard; American minds could never understand what they understood. For this knowledge, they were well paid. They had learned to depend upon this pay for comforts others did not enjoy. We were certain the native police boys were with us both in mind and body and would fight for us to the death if necessary.

When we hit the trail again, we were more cautious than we had been previously. Elston had placed the police boys in what he thought to be the best position. Two of them marched at the head of the column with rifles loaded and cocked. This is where their knowledge of the jungle was critical. Their eyes constantly searched the forward line of march and each side of the trail. We were a small party compared to the potential enemy we faced, but the way Elston had our defense set up made us a formidable foe.

Elston was still leading the carriers, stopping every few hundred yards to look through his field glasses. He searched the surrounding terrain for the slightest unnatural movement in the kunai grass.

Had we not been in uncontrolled territory I would have considered this afternoon walk a pleasant one. My body, passing the point of endurance, seemed to have adapted to the rigors of the trek. Or perhaps it was because in hostile territory we had to remain constantly alert. Our lives depended upon our alertness, agility, sharpness, and stealth. Fear allowed us to forget our aches and pains.

We were skirting a mountain that reared its ragged head at an elevation of more than eight thousand feet. The slippery trail began at a ravine, one thousand feet from the mountaintop and wound about the mountain like a treacherous snake. The stream in the ravine glistened as it crashed against the boulders obstructing its path. The afternoon sun gave the brown kunai grass a golden appearance not unlike the waving wheat fields of Kansas, and the trees were so green that they gave the impression of having been freshly painted. The stream looked cool and refreshing; I am sure every man there considered plunging in. I have never seen a more beautiful sight.

The narrow, rocky footpath we followed tilted at a thirty-degree angle. A wrong step meant a plunge from a one-thousand-foot-high cliff into the river below. My number one boy was as sure-footed as a mountain goat. He led me along the path, almost dragging me at times. I made good use of the cane Elston had given me. The police boys and our personal aides stood by, ready to assist us if necessary.

Our dangerous walk ended at a plateau overlooking a vast yellow valley, a Shangri-La in the heart of the jungle. The tall kunai grass bent in the cool breeze. Smoke rising from the village below curled up over the mountain. I thought it strange that a country so beautiful should be inhabited by a people so savage that they ate other human beings.

The trail leading down the mountain, the first trail we had seen all day, was smooth. It didn't take us long to get to the bottom of the valley.

At four o'clock in the afternoon we arrived at a beautiful spot surrounded by huge trees. One of the police boys informed Elston that the village was named Tunofi. He had heard about it from other natives by way of the "native telegraph," as Elston chose to call it. The speed at which news could travel in the jungle was amazing. It was almost as fast as the radio!

Posting the police boys with their loaded rifles in a large circle around us, we lay down on the cool grass. We weren't there long before natives came toward us bearing armloads of food. Few of them wore any clothing. Most of the men had their genitals tied up in leaves or protected by a piece of seashell or gourd. The children were completely naked, except for a bracelet or arm band.

The Tunofi natives appeared quite relaxed. But they were not as friendly as the New Guineans we had encountered in controlled territory. They did not greet our bearers and police boys with the traditional genital caress.

"You never can tell, Ed," Elston cautioned as he watched the procession of headhunters approaching. "You see, there are no Marys with them. They're not sure whether or not they're going to attack us. They're coming under the peaceful guise of bearing gifts to see what our strength is and how well we're armed. Perhaps they'll go back and not bother us at all; on the other hand, they may deposit their food at our feet and go back to the village for their weapons."

As the Tunofis stood outside the circle of our police boys I caressed the handle of my .45. I knew one man who wasn't going to be caught napping.

Finally Elston yelled something in Pidgin English and the police boys waved the fierce-looking natives into the circle. The porters, reluctant at first, refused to mingle with the Tunofis.

"It's all right, Major," Elston said. "They're not armed, at least not the ones we can see. They won't do any harm. I think they really just came to trade food."

"They've never seen a white man?"

"I doubt it."

"Then why aren't they staring at us instead of trying to trade food with our boys?"

"I don't know," Elston said. "But if I were you, I wouldn't seek too much publicity from them. You're liable to find yourself in their soup pot!

"The native may work his Mary to death," Elston continued. "But he'll also protect her with his life. At the first sign of danger, he'll hide her in a safe place and face that danger alone. A group of natives without their Marys is bad news. The scene might not be as peaceful as it seems on the surface."

"But all the men out here are unarmed," I said. "What would they fight with?"

"Don't think for a minute that every Tunofi man is out here trading with us," he warned.

"Are there more?" I asked, realizing how unaware I was.

"We're probably completely surrounded at this very moment." There was no reason for me to doubt Elston, but I hoped our situation wasn't as bad as he made it sound.

The trading session lasted about thirty minutes. When it was over, a few Marys appeared out of nowhere to join the natives. The tension among our group eased somewhat, and soon the Tunofis departed.

It was still quite early in the day and the sun was fairly high, but in another two hours it would be dark. Brady and Lock stood gazing at the quiet, clear stream that flowed near where we were camped. It was rather wide, perhaps twenty-five feet, open on the side where we stood, but fringed with dense brush on the far bank.

"Jack, how would it be if Lock and I took a swim?" Brady asked.

Elston thought for a moment and then turned to Timms, "I see no objections, Gil, if they want to cool off a bit. What do you think?"

"If they take a couple of police boys to stand guard it should be safe. Have them stand on the other side of the stream near the bushes and tell them to stay alert."

Brady and Lock nodded and went over to where Lee Mills was conversing in Pidgin English with the police boys. They said something to Mills and a moment later two police boys left the group and followed the two American officers toward the stream. The native boys waded to the other side of the river and stood on the bank, where they could see the swimmers at all times. Lock and Brady took off all their clothes and waded in. We could hear their laughter and I thought about how nice it would be to cool off. A few moments later, I was splashing in the water beside them.

We had only been in the water about ten minutes when suddenly there was a commotion on the bank where the brush was thickest. Three naked natives stood poised with bows drawn and arrows aimed straight at us. I yelled at the top of my voice, "Get underwater!" My two companions understood right away and got under as far as the shallow water would permit.

After a minute underwater, I felt that my lungs would burst. I couldn't stand it any longer. Turning my body until I thought I would be facing the bank where I had seen the natives, I poked my head out of the water far enough for my nose to be above the surface. I took a deep breath, drawing fresh air into my straining lungs. Sixty seconds underwater had seemed like a lifetime. I almost sank when I finally opened my eyes and saw a barbed arrow slowly floating downstream.

There was a struggle in the bushes across the river. The two native police boys appeared, shoving the three naked natives who had tried to kill us. One police boy shoved a native down into the mud when the native tried to balk. Then he helped the native to his feet and shoved him again. This time, the native didn't balk.

On the opposite bank, our native bearers and police boys jabbered excitedly and pointed at the captives. Some of the men from Tunofi, including the chief, had joined the crowd.

When the police boys and their captives reached the river bank, the captives turned and attacked their captors. Using their rifle butts, the police boys beat them severely. Blood flowed out of the captives' noses; one had a nasty cut across his face.

Brady, Lock, and I scampered out of the water as fast as we could and put on our clothes. The police boys shoved the would-be assassins across the stream and brought them into camp where they stood, sullen and stoic. The police boys surrounded the captives and motioned for the other natives to stand back. Our men held their rifles at readiness and I had my hand on the butt of my pistol. Lock got a rifle and slammed a shell into the chamber, but Elston didn't even reach for his gun. He walked up to the native who appeared to be in charge of the group and began speaking to him in Pidgin English.

Apparently, Elston was threatening to execute the three natives who had tried to kill us because the savages began to shake and mutter. Then they began to howl in the most mournful tones I had ever heard. Elston apparently was now giving the chief a severe tongue-lashing.

Finally, Timms came over to translate for me. "Jack has the chief going. We were on a friendly mission and wanted peace, he's complaining, and yet our lives were threatened for no reason. He's giving the chief the third degree and explaining that we have weapons that can wipe out his entire village in minutes if he doesn't tell his boys to back off."

The natives eventually calmed down and the men who had tried to attack us stopped shaking. Elston glared at the chief, left him, and came over to me.

"The whole thing happened because the natives thought we were after them," he explained. "They were trying to prevent us from going any farther into their territory, but I think it's all right now."

"I hope so," I said unsteadily.

"We can't let down our guard," Elston warned. "There might be more trouble. These natives are extremely territorial. I think the chief will try to keep his men under control. But you never can tell if a group might break away from the village, go against the chief's orders, and attack us.

"Now you've seen it for yourselves," Elston said. "These people are headhunters; they'll kill you."

IX
SING-SING

The realization that some of us had come so close to death set my nerves on edge. Fighting the Japanese was one thing, but fighting hidden natives armed with bows and arrows — silent weapons — was another.

The natives of the Papuan plains and western mountains of New Guinea use arrows tipped with bamboo or bone points. The fighting arrows are usually fitted with a loose head which becomes detached in a wound. The foreshaft of the arrow is generally covered with bone fragments smeared with a latex mixture. The latex dissolves in the wound, allowing the bones to imbed themselves in the body. If proper medical attention is immediately available, serious complications may be avoided. In our present situation, the dangers to our party were great.

Elston wandered about for some time talking in Pidgin English with the natives. Everyone relaxed and our police boys began bargaining with the headhunters. Soon the atmosphere was almost pleasant. Elston informed me that he had told the chief that unless we were granted safe passage through his country, we would kill many of his warriors. He had explained that we were well armed, but that — above all else — we wanted to travel in peace. The chief had given his word that we would not be harmed while we were within his jurisdiction, but he could not guarantee our safety beyond those limits.

Even though Elston assured me that we were safe while we camped near this village, I could not feel safe when we had so recently been threatened. These people are savages — I thought, what was to prevent another episode like the earlier one?

But evidently Elston had been persuasive. Marys eventually joined the assembled Tunofi, which was a sure sign that the hostilities had ended. These women wore even less clothing than the women we had seen at Bena Bena. They were completely nude above the waist and were barely covered below it.

The men were the wildest, fiercest, most ferocious-looking natives I had seen. Their noses were pierced with long tusks. I wondered how they could breathe, since the tusks almost completely clogged their nasal passages. Some of them wore feathers in their hair or adorned their heads with cassowary quills, which gave the impression of hair standing straight up on the top of the head. A gourd fastened to their waists with string made of strong kunai grass covered and protected their genitals. Their greased bodies reeked of pig fat; their voices were guttural, from another world. Never having been encased in shoes, their broad feet looked like paddles. The nails of their thick toes had been partially worn away. I had seen people like these nowhere else on earth.

When Elston informed us that the chief had been persuaded to hold a sing-sing in our honor, I knew that we had made peace with the tribe. The sing-sing began at dusk with the natives chanting and dancing in wild ecstasy. There was no music; the natives created a harmony and rhythm with their voices. To me their song was as monotonous as the steady drip, drip, drip of a leaky faucet. It was very loud in the beginning, but the volume tapered off as the hours passed. Finally, only a soft drone could be heard as the natives slowly drifted back to their village, one by one.

We slept with our clothes on and kept our loaded .45s within reach. I reminded everyone that if Mother Nature called we should answer her within the confines of our camp. Two police boys patrolled the area outside our tent while another circled the camp area. We were taking no chances, despite the chief's assurances of peace.

Toward morning, as I was finally beginning to sleep soundly, I was awakened by one of our police boys. He came running into our tent shouting, "Master! Master!" Then he went to Elston's sleeping bag and shook him, yelling again, "Master! Master!"

Elston opened his eyes and stared blankly at the black man in the dim light. He too had only been asleep for a short time and woke up quite confused and startled. "What is it, boy?" he said. "What's the matter?"

"*Master, Kanaka belong Hahagini em he kaikai altogether this fella Master he fall down onetime baluus.*" Translation: the white man who crashed in the plane was eaten by the Hahagini tribe.

By this time we were all wide-awake. This tragic news was what we had dreaded; our most horrible thoughts had become reality.

Elston scrambled out of his sleeping bag and confronted the native police boy. "How did you get this information, boy? Tell me!"

"By native telegraph, Master."

"Are they holding this native prisoner?"

"I do not know, Master."

"Go back to your post and find out whatever you can about where this man can be located. If you hear anything, report back to me immediately." There was excitement in Elston's voice now, and he was more upset than I had ever heard him.

"Yes, Master," the native said, and departed quickly. Although the conversation between the native and Elston had been in Pidgin English, all of us understood enough to get the general idea. When Elston turned to us he sounded somewhat puzzled, as if he were not sure how to break the news.

"You have to take this report with a grain of salt," he said. "The natives have a habit of telling you what they think you want to hear. I think that's what's happening in this case. There is a great deal of jealousy among tribes, and stories like this often spread as an act of revenge."

"You mean they would start rumors just to cause trouble for a neighbor?" I asked.

"It's happened before," Elston said. "I would rather you didn't jump to any conclusions."

"Jack, I think you're too cautious," I said. "Eating humans is nothing new to these natives. Seems to me they could have thought of a better story than this one if revenge is what they were after."

"I won't say you're right and I won't say you're wrong," Elston said. "But I know what will happen the moment a native admits he's eaten an American . . ."

". . . or an Aussie," Lock interrupted.

"Or an Aussie," Elston added. "Lock, you'd split his head with a bullet. Right?"

"Righto," Lock said. "That would be too good for him."

Timms, who had been listening to the conversation, rolled over and propped his head up on his elbow. "Gents, there's another way to look at it. You see, we're not in Australia or America now. We're in uncontrolled territory. These people have never been taught an ounce of civilized ways. What they know has been handed down to them from generation to generation and they know nothing else. In America and Australia, there are certain laws which govern the conduct of the people; here they have laws, too, only their laws are much different.

"If we were to kill a native we would be asked, 'Why?' We would answer, 'Because he ate a white man.' Do you know what the chief's answer would be? 'We have eaten human flesh for as long as we can remember. It tastes good and it's easy to obtain. Besides, what's the difference between eating a native and eating a white man?'"

"We could explain that it simply isn't done in our country," I interjected.

"You're not in your country, Ed. You're in their country. And, if I may say so, you may have to follow some of their rules if you intend to stay alive. That's putting it rather crudely, I'm sure; nevertheless, that's the way it is."

In spite of Timms's point of view, I couldn't resign myself to letting a guilty cannibal off scot-free. That just wasn't my idea of justice. If I had the chance to avenge wronged Americans, I knew I would do it. I was sure the other Americans would be right behind me.

With Timms's words still ringing in my ears, I lay back down. I reached for my .45 with a sweaty hand and patted it gently. It was reassuring to know it was near. I rolled over and tried to sleep, but I couldn't. My blood was boiling. Although the early morning was cold, I had broken out in a sweat. What a way to die, I thought.

I didn't sleep the rest of the morning. When it began to grow light outside, I suddenly became conscious of someone standing close to my sleeping bag. I grabbed my .45, thumbed back the hammer, and whirled around. The cook stood next to me, holding a cup of hot tea. When he saw the gun he almost dropped the scalding liquid on me, but when I let down the hammer and put the gun down, his face broke into a huge smile.

As the cook placed the cup of tea beside me on the ground, he shrugged his shoulders as if to say, "Bad dream, maybe?"

It was six in the morning and the sun was peeking over the mountains in the distance. I looked outside at the orange sky streaked with tinges of red and yellow. Little patches of fog hung in the curves of the hills.

Everyone was unusually quiet that morning, including the native porters, who were usually cheerful and chatty. I wondered if they weren't contemplating throwing our supplies to the ground and deserting us. As crude and uncivilized as their homes were, uncontrolled territory was even worse. At least in controlled territory they knew what to expect.

The rumor of cannibalism had done something to all of us. Though we had known that cannibalism was common, the threat of it had never been more real.

However, since the police boy who had brought the jarring

news was unable to obtain any convincing details to substantiate the grisly story, there was hope it was simply a malicious rumor.

I had only one thing to be grateful for that morning. I had become accustomed to the rigorous walking. My legs and joints were not as sore and stiff as they had been on previous mornings. For this I was thankful.

My arms, though, were still terribly sore and my beard bothered me. My pith helmet covered my face fairly well, but not enough to keep out the burning sun. The combination of sunburn and itchy whiskers was painful, but it was nothing compared to the way my legs had felt.

The trail we walked over was quite irregular and wound up and down mountains which were at least a thousand feet high. We were walking at an average elevation of about sixty-five hundred feet. At the bottom of each mountain there was always a stream. Some of them were narrow enough to jump across and others were so wide we had to be carried across by the natives. Not once did a native grumble at the heavy load he was forced to carry across these torrential streams.

Shortly before noon our party was descending a thickly wooded mountainside streaked with small rivulets and streams. The passage was extremely difficult because the ground was damp and slippery. It was probably the slowest we had moved since the start of the trek. A native police boy ran to the back of the line. He came up to me, a scared look on his face, and whispered excitedly in Pidgin English, "Master Jack sent me back to tell you there might be trouble ahead. He sees natives in the bush."

"Go back and tell Master Jack I'll be up with him in a minute. Hurry, now."

The boy darted off. I didn't have to warn Lock and Brady. Overhearing the native boy's warning, Lock pulled back the bolt on his rifle and rammed home a shell. Brady had taken his own gun from its holster and stood fingering it.

"Don't you guys shoot until you're told to," I warned them.

"If we kill one native needlessly, we've had it."

Lock and Brady nodded, but I wasn't certain I had convinced them. Telling my number one and number two boys to stay where they were, I ran toward Elston. I lost my footing several times and slipped in the mud, plastering my already-dirty trousers with muck.

Just as I reached Elston a shower of arrows sailed over our heads. I heard them thud into the ground. I heard a scream and Elston yelled, "Get down low and ready your guns!"

Elston and I lay side by side on the muddy path. He placed his field glasses to his eyes and squinted. "My God, Ed! Take a look!"

I did, and then I wished I hadn't. There were natives everywhere on the small hill opposite us. I could see them crawling like black ants, each one carrying a bow and several barbed arrows. Handing the glasses back to Elston, I put my gun to my shoulder, determined to make a stand. Elston shouted to a police boy, who set up the Bren gun. Then Elston waved for two other police boys to come to us. "Go get a hostage," he said in Pidgin English. "Quickly!"

The boys left hurriedly, slipping into the brush and out of sight. "What good is one hostage when the hills are full of savages?" I asked Elston. "It seems stupid to sacrifice two police boys!"

"You'll see," he said, fingering the Bren gun. "We'll hold our fire until we see what the boys bring back. If they're not successful we may have to fight our way out . . . if we can."

"I'm for doing it now. By the time the police boys take a hostage, the natives will have us surrounded."

"They have a strong herd instinct, Ed. If we can capture one tribesman the natives will stop firing."

"It doesn't seem likely that people who have so little regard for human life will stop a war to save one life."

"You wouldn't think so, Ed, but I've been told by Aussies who've had encounters with hostile tribesmen that this method works."

Brady and Lock came up and sprawled out beside us. The natives had not fired since the first volley. I wondered if it had been just a warning.

"I'm for shooting our way through those beasts," Brady said. "They can't stand up against our bullets with bows and arrows."

"Take it easy," I warned.

"Yes, Lieutenant," Elston said. "Let's just lie here quietly and see what they're up to. They have us outnumbered ten to one. I'd like to shoot the bloody creatures down like dogs too, but the odds are against us. This is their country and they know how to fight in it."

Brady fingered the trigger of his gun, a disgusted look on his face. "Hogwash. Kill a few and take the fight out of them."

"Brady, you'll do as Elston says. That's an order," I said.

"Fine, Major," he said sarcastically. "Maybe you'd like to know what that scream was when the arrows were fired at us."

"The scream? What, did one of the natives get scared?"

"They got scared, all right. Gil is back there now threatening to shoot them if they try to head for the bush."

"Gil will handle them," Elston said.

"I hope he knows how to handle dead ones, too."

"Dead ones?" I asked. "What dead ones?"

"Your number two boy. He got an arrow right through the head."

X
BURIAL

I didn't wait to ask more questions. Leaping up, I ran headlong down the slippery path. When I reached the rear of the line, there was a group of carriers and a police boy gathered around my number two boy. Timms stood nearby with his gun held at the ready, guarding the mournful group.

Shoving aside the circle of men, I knelt beside the small, limp body of the eight-year-old boy whom I had liked and trusted so much. The shaft of a barbed arrow stuck out of his head. About three inches of it had penetrated through the side of his skull just forward of his left ear. I took out my knife and cut the shaft off as close to his head as possible. I picked up the lifeless body and held it in my arms. The natives scattered and sat down on the ground. Because the arrows had stopped and they knew that Elston had sent for a hostage, they were no longer afraid.

I looked down into the blank face of the little native who had carried my camera with all the dignity of a gun bearer. His eyes would no longer sparkle and dance when I pretended to be angry with him. I would no longer hear his musical laughter as he jogged along the trail, gladly running my errands from one end of the line to the other. He had never complained or been sullen. He was a mere child. He wanted to be grown-up. He had proven to be grown-up in many ways; he could carry his share of the load and walk as far as the others.

Now he would never have the chance to grow up. My number two boy lay in my arms as if he were asleep. I had seen men die before, but I had never seen a child die. I couldn't stop the tears from flowing. They dripped onto the little black body and glistened on his skin. It was the only tribute I could pay to the gallant little fellow who had served me so well.

After a few minutes, I placed him gently on the ground. "Gil, I said, "we'll have to bury him here. We can't take him back."

"I know, Ed."

"We'll have to explain to his people."

"Jack will take care of that," Timms said. "I'm sure he's had to do it before. Don't worry about it, Ed. I'll have the natives bury him."

Leaving Timms with the boy, I made my way back to the head of the line, almost a quarter of a mile away. Police boys patrolled the line to protect the porters and our supplies, and most of the porters were flattened out on the ground to keep themselves from becoming targets. Elston, who still had the Bren gun set up, was lying on the ground nearby. Brady and Lock lay quietly, their guns at the ready. I lay down between Brady and Elston, cocked my rifle, and snugged my cheek against the stock.

"You don't have to go that far, Ed," Elston said. "I don't think there'll be any more trouble."

"I hope not, Jack. My number two boy is dead. The first native with ill intent who crosses my sights has had it."

"You'd only be asking for trouble, Ed. You must listen to me."

"I'm listening, but I think there's only one way to resolve this."

When Elston looked over at me his eyes were blazing. "You fire one shot and we'll never get out of here alive," he warned. "I know these natives."

A black form suddenly entered my sights. I took careful aim, my finger tightening on the trigger, but I realized that my target was one of our own police boys.

In the next instant two frightened police boys came into the clearing half-carrying, half-dragging a panicked captive. He was fighting wildly, babbling words I could not understand.

Elston looked over at me. "It's all right, Ed. Everything's all right. Now let's see what this native's got to say."

Approaching the hostage, Elston flew into a rage. He demanded that the native sing out to his tribesmen, telling them to lay down their weapons and go back to their village. If they didn't do as Elston told them, he would kill them all with his magic "thing of the noise."

The native quieted down and looked sullenly at Elston, who was touching his .45. Again and again Elston told his captive to sing out, but the native remained silent, refusing to say a word. When Elston drew his .45 from its holster, the native's eyes grew wider, but he soon regained his mask of defiance. Elston prodded him with the gun, yet the native continued to ignore him.

Gripping the handle of the .45 firmly, Elston lashed out, hitting his captive just above the right ear. Blood flowed from the gash, dripping from the savage's chin and running down his chest. Fear filled his eyes.

"Sing out!" Elston screamed. "Sing out loud!"

Elston brought the pistol barrel down again, this time on top of the cannibal's head. The man staggered and his knees gave out. I expected him to collapse at any moment. Again and again, Elston struck him. The captive was able to evade some of the blows, but others he caught full-force. Finally, the battered captive could no longer control himself. He began defecating on the ground. I couldn't take any more and walked away. The native probably couldn't understand why he was being tortured for the entire tribe.

After a moment I turned toward Elston. "That's enough, Jack!" I said. "Stop it immediately!"

Elston paused, glared at me for an instant, then turned away. He started beating the native again. Suddenly, the native began to sing out loud, wailing as if he were mourning for the dead. His face and head were a huge mass of cuts and bruises. Blood washed his body and ran to the ground, where small red puddles formed in the mud. The sight was so sickening, I thought I might vomit. Brady, Lock, and the others had walked away and were standing with their backs to the awful scene.

As the man sang out, several of his tribesmen straggled in from the bush, surrendering without their weapons. Elston yelled at them to return for their weapons and meet us at the small village we could see in the distance. He warned that if they continued to make trouble, we would kill the hostage. Elston turned the captive over to the police boys and came over to me.

"It wasn't nice, was it?" he asked.

"It looked to me as if you actually enjoyed it, Jack."

"Enjoy that? No man enjoys that sort of thing. There are many things you need to learn if you expect to remain alive in the jungle, Ed. If that native hadn't sung out when he did, there's no telling what would have happened. Our lives were hanging in the balance there for a moment. These people aren't fooling around."

I knew that Elston was right. It wasn't in his nature to torture another human being. He did what he had to do, knowing that the natives' loyalty would save our lives.

Lee Mills touched my arm. "Ed, Gil and the natives buried your number two boy."

"Did they mark the grave?"

"I don't know."

"Do me a favor, Lee. Go back and ask Gil to make a small cross and stick it into the ground. Will you do that, Lee?"

"Sure, Ed. No sweat."

I was liking Mills more all the time. He was understanding and brave.

We went to the village, taking the captive with us. The natives had started coming back with their weapons. The women and children stood off to the side, showing no emotion. One by one, the native men carried their weapons to the center of the circle of huts and put them on the ground as Elston had directed. Then they stood by the women, sullen, frightened, and quiet.

For the next half hour Elston, Timms, and the police boys searched each hut in the village for evidence that these natives had been to the crash site. But aside from a few pigs, they found nothing, not even a stalk of sugar cane.

After the search, Elston looked at the stack of weapons, then stood in the center of the circle. In his Pidgin English he warned those assembled that any further attempts to harm us would result in severe punishment. He advised them that the Australian government — an entity that probably few, if any, had ever heard of — might even condemn the village leaders to death.

Although Elston's speech was convincing, we all knew that if we killed one native the tribe would retaliate. This was our second encounter with hostile natives and we had made it this far without firing a shot. I wondered how long our luck would last.

After Elston's speech we released the captive. Two huge men rushed to get him and took him inside one of the huts. A Mary left the group of silent women and followed them. Elston motioned for us to assemble the party again and be on our way, while the natives were still compliant. I wasn't concerned about our immediate safety, but I was worried about our return trip through this village. The Dunantina River tribe was fierce and territorial, and would no doubt be awaiting our return, prepared for battle. Their scouts would keep them posted on our progress via the native telegraph, so they would know every move we made from the time we started back until the moment we arrived at their doorstep.

When we hit the trail again it was with a great deal of relief. I was still mourning the little native boy we had buried. But I forced myself to focus on the task at hand. I knew there would be more of the same, or worse, ahead of us, so I had to remain alert.

After we had been on the trail for more than an hour, we came to a river about fifty feet wide. Across it was strung a bamboo bridge. While waiting for the porters to cross, Brady, Reed, and McGovern went for a swim, but not until we had posted several police boys at strategic points to prevent a recurrence of earlier events. We decided to eat lunch there since it was already noon. The spot was cool and shady under a canopy of tall trees and jungle vines, and the beauty of the colorful birds and the sandy stream helped everyone relax. It amazed me that the jungle could be both peaceful and frightening at the same time.

We plodded on for the remainder of the afternoon. The country seemed less rugged and the hike was much easier. We were all doing much better, both mentally and physically. At times I wondered how Reed and McGovern — the senior citizens of our group — managed to keep up with the rest of the party. Neither one of them spoke much as we walked. I figured they were saving their strength for what was ahead. Despite their pain and exhaustion, neither of them griped.

By early evening we had reached a small village called Amorika. Sending one of the policemen ahead to the village to advise the headman of our peaceful intentions, we made camp nearby. The natives of Amorika had probably heard about what had happened at the last village. There were no Marys in sight when we arrived, but the men appeared peaceful. Still, Elston would not relax his vigil. I had learned to trust his judgment, so I was careful not to let my guard down either.

In Amorika the natives told us that the airplane had crashed only a few miles away, and that we were about a day's march from the crash site. Elston suggested we camp for the night and take up our search for the wreckage the next day. I had no desire to spend another night so close to a headhunter village. It was plain from the expressions on the others' faces that they shared my feelings, but no one objected to Elston's suggestion. We depended on him for guidance. In the middle of hostile country we had to rely on Elston, Timms, and Mills. As far as we were concerned, they knew more about New Guinea than any other white men alive.

As we set up camp about a hundred yards from the village, I imagined I could see arrow points sticking out of the bush, aimed straight at our hearts — but none came.

XI

AMORIKA VILLAGE

Walking around the camp with Mills, I came upon the remains of a campfire that had apparently been abandoned for several days. Mills poked his cane into the charred ashes and suddenly struck something hard. Stooping down, he picked up a blackened object.

"Beat this if you can, chap," he said to me. "Here's a human skull with a fairly good set of teeth."

Mills offered the skull to me but I took a step backwards. "I really don't care to handle it, Lee. You keep it," I said.

"Looks like he's only been dead a few days — young native, I'd say. What say we have a little fun?"

"How?"

"With Brady. He's been on edge lately. Perhaps a joke will improve his attitude."

"Suits me."

Mills carried the skull to our tent. There was no one else there. We placed the gruesome thing in Brady's bag. Since he hadn't unpacked his clothing to air, we knew that he was likely to do so upon returning to the tent.

After planting the skull, we went outside where the rest of the men were gathered in a bull session. Gil Timms was lecturing about cannibalism.

Timms explained that the Papuans, as a rule, are a territorial people who are hostile to strangers. Sometimes they even go to war with their closest neighbors. During the early phases of the Australian mandate, the Aussies taught many of the natives in controlled territory to give up cannibalism. But this only occurred in the fringe areas; in central Papua, cannibalism was still practiced. Human flesh was simply regarded as another source of food in these areas. Early explorers to this region reported that strangers and neighboring tribes were the prime source of human flesh.

"Cannibalism isn't actually their first choice," Timms continued. "Papuans eat human flesh only when it's impossible to get meat from another source. If you remember, nearly every village we went through had a few dozen pigs; but when there are no pigs and no birds, the natives substitute human flesh. There's a common expression among headhunters: '*Meat belong masta e all a same pig.*' In other words, 'Man's flesh tastes just like pig's meat.'"

"Have you ever eaten human flesh, Gil?" Brady asked.

"Are you accusing me of cannibalism?"

"No. I was just wondering."

"Well, I haven't," Timms said.

I didn't care what Timms had done during his lengthy stay in New Guinea. He had lived under extreme hardship at times. Maybe he had been in a situation where he had had to eat another human being's flesh to survive. No one would have blamed him if he had admitted to that. I hoped Brady would drop the subject, but he didn't.

"Would you eat it if you were starving to death?" Brady asked. He slid closer to Timms.

"I sure would, and I'm sure you would too if you were desperate," Timms replied. "It's easy to say you wouldn't, but if you were desperate . . ."

"You've been here too long, Timms. Any man who would eat another human is, in my opinion . . ."

"Is what, in your opinion?" Timms asked angrily.

"I'd rather starve than eat human flesh," answered Brady, reserving his judgment.

"If you didn't know what it was, you'd eat it. You'd probably even like it. What's wrong with human flesh? It's clean and it'll keep you alive."

"A man has to have scruples," Brady said. "He has to draw the line, and eating human flesh is beyond that line."

"Speaking of scruples," Elston interrupted, "would you believe that these natives will eat their own mothers and fathers?"

"Right now I'd believe anything," Brady answered.

"A native will eat a member of his own tribe, even a member of his own family, if that person has distinguished himself in some way," Elston continued. "If a tribesman has lived long and wisely and has become an honored member of the community, there will be a feast at his death. All the natives will eat a piece of his body in an effort to acquire some of his good qualities."

"I'll make certain that none of them take a liking to me," Brady said. "What kind of people do they like? Fat, muscular, or skinny?"

"Well, I don't know. Maybe they don't have any preference. Why?"

"I was thinking of Reed. He won't have any trouble with cannibals. There's no meat on him."

"There'll be even less if we walk much farther," Reed growled.

"I've had enough of this cannibalism business for one day," I said.

Brady got up. "So have I. Personally, Jack, I wish you and Gil would keep that kind of talk to yourselves from now on. We've got enough to think about without getting all worked up over headhunters."

Timms looked up and pointed a finger at Brady. "Oh, I say, Lieutenant, there's one more thing I have to mention to make the dissertation complete: Papuans will eat human flesh no matter what the cause of death may be — even flesh from people who died of syphilis, leprosy, or any other infectious disease. So you see, Lieutenant Brady, no one can escape the blade of the headhunter!"

"Go to hell," Brady answered, walking away in disgust. Timms and Elston had probably gone too far with young Brady.

"I hope I didn't make the chap too angry," Timms said, when Brady was out of earshot. "He's been rather touchy today. He's really drawn himself into his shell."

The morbid discussion about cannibalism disturbed me. A hike through lush forests and jungles, high mountains, and deep gorges would have been pleasant under other circumstances. But the headhunter factor made the difficult voyage through this land a waking nightmare. I began to regret the prank that Mills had prepared for Brady.

Suddenly a blood-curdling scream echoed from the tent — Brady had discovered the skull.

I got up and ran to him. "Easy, boy. What's the matter?" He was visibly frightened.

"Back there. There's a head inside my bag. A head without hair or a body!"

"Where'd it come from?" I asked, trying to look calm.

"Hell, Major, how should I know? All I know is that I opened the bag and there it was staring at me. Come and see for yourself," he said.

Mills and I followed him into the tent. "I'm ready to pull out of this stinking mess right now!" Brady yelled.

"Now settle down, Lieutenant," Mills said. "This thing's been dead for days. The major and I thought we'd play a little joke on you. You know, try to liven up the situation a bit. What say we forget the whole thing, brace up, and make the best of the rest of the trip? You know, one sour grape can ruin the bunch."

Brady — huge, muscular Brady — finally grinned at Mills and me. "Already forgotten. No sweat . . . now where are those cook boys? I'm hungry!"

Mills picked up the skull and handed it to Brady. "Your dinner, Lieutenant," he said with a completely straight face.

The episode helped break the tension; everyone seemed pretty relaxed at dinner. We had a plan: if we were attacked during the night, the porters were to head for cover in a designated area so they wouldn't be in our line of fire. We doubled the police guard around the camp as night fell.

We had supper by the light from a kerosene lamp. Sitting around in a large circle, we gorged ourselves on *kau-kau*, fresh corn, and beans we had gotten from the last tribe we had encountered. We also had our old standby of cheese and biscuits. We'd be thankful for the protein and carbohydrates on our walk the next day. The cook boys carrying platters of food cast weird shadows on the tent wall, and several times I found my hand creeping for my gun.

Crawling into my sleeping bag, my gun close by, I folded my arms under my head and stared up into the darkness. If we ever got out of this place in one piece, I thought, we'd be telling these stories back home. Our hardships would be magnified, the mountains would tower higher, the valleys would be steeper, and the streams more treacherous. But even imagination could not prepare me for what was to come.

XII
CRASH SITE

I awoke the next morning after an excellent night's sleep. In less than four hours, we would reach the crash site and complete our mission. Perhaps we would find what was left of the airmen, perhaps not. The natives might have already "taken care" of the bodies.

Our orders were to bury the remains of the flyers and return to Bena Bena. Of course, we were also to determine whether any of the men had been cannibalized.

Suppose we did uncover evidence that the headhunters had cannibalized our crew members? Suppose we could prove it conclusively? Was I supposed to go back and tell the general the whole truth, knowing he would try to blast the natives from the hills as a result?

I suddenly realized that the hostile natives were not the biggest challenge I faced. If I learned that American airmen had been cannibalized, I would be faced with a decision far more formidable than anything I had encountered in the bush.

My thoughts were interrupted by Elston's voice yelling in Pidgin English at the native porters. He was telling them to shoulder their packs for the last leg of our journey. When Elston gave the order, we lined up and began walking. I walked rather reluctantly, dreading the task before us, the job we had come to do.

After climbing for almost three hours, we called a halt and gathered at the crest of a mountain. To our left, about two thousand feet below us and nearly four miles away, a small, peaceful-looking village lay, disturbed only by a few wisps of smoke that curled up from cooking fires. The land was beautiful. The mountain ridges on the distant horizon looked like steps of stone in a giant rock garden. The clearings on the numerous hillsides formed a pattern of Mother Nature's own knitting. The green trees, white waterfalls, and multicolored rocks all blended with the rich, black soil. This serene beauty lay on our left, while on our right, deep in the heart of a valley, lay a tangled mass of wreckage and the object of our mission — the crashed American bomber.

It took almost an hour to reach the site from the crest of the ridge. As we stood looking at the mass of twisted metal, I wondered how we could possibly determine what had caused the crash. In an area of about thirty square yards lay the largest part of the 100,000-pound four-engine bomber, so completely mangled that we could hardly distinguish the fuselage from the other parts of the craft. The wings were intact; only slightly damaged by the impact of the crash.

Brady, McGovern, Reed, and I began the task of sifting through the debris in an attempt to discover a possible cause for the crash and to assemble the skeletal remains of the crew. We had to certify that the number of crew members matched the number of skeletons found. The task was not only gruesome, but arduous as well, because there was so much ground to be covered.

The position of the bomber's wings indicated that the plane had hit the ground in an almost perpendicular descent. This led me to believe that the wings of the aircraft were intact until the craft crashed and had only separated from the fuselage on impact. The bombs on board the aircraft probably exploded on impact, completely destroying the fuselage and killing the entire crew. If this explosion theory were true, there wouldn't have been much human flesh for the cannibals to eat.

After an hour of work, I sent Brady out into the surrounding area with two police boys to try to locate the tail section of the aircraft. I also asked Elston to try to make contact with some locals, so we could determine if there were any eyewitnesses with information regarding the path, altitude, and condition of the aircraft prior to the crash.

About an hour and a half later, Brady returned with six of our carriers, the native police boys, and sections of the vertical fin, rudder, and horizontal stabilizer.

"We found these parts of the tail assembly about one-half mile south of here, Ed," he said.

Before making a detailed inspection of the tail assembly of the bomber, I looked at the vertical stabilizer, the rudders, the horizontal stabilizer, and the elevators. I was trying to recall details from my metallurgy and aircraft maintenance classes. I was more comfortable and confident about this task, since it was much more in line with my aviation training and experience.

I was trying to picture the chain of events which caused the crash. Unlike the wings, the tail assembly showed no evidence of impact, fire, or heat damage. The fact that the complete tail assembly separated prior to impact was especially troubling. The tail assembly required a more detailed study.

Using a magnifying glass, I proceeded to inspect the stabilizer, then the elevators, then the vertical fins. I found an astonishing bit of evidence on the vertical fin. The four bolts that held the rudders in place had been severed. The forged bolts, which were made of "chrom-molly" steel, a composite of chromium and molybdenum, one of the world's strongest metals, had sheared, causing the rudder to separate from the aircraft. My tentative conclusion was that the loss of lateral control that resulted when the rudder tore away from the vertical fin also damaged the elevators, causing them to fail.

The airplane therefore went into an uncontrolled, near-vertical descent. The fact that the debris from the crash of this large bomber covered only thirty square yards supported this theory.

In the normal service of aircraft, metal parts seldom fail because of fracture or stress under a single load or even a few loads of maximum intensity. Parts, especially for aircraft, are pretested before installation. When failure occurs in the early stages of flight operations, a redesign of the part with stronger material is immediately commissioned. However, fatigue failures can occur at calculated loads. These fatigue failures occur only after loads have been repeated many times.

Since fatigue can occur without noticeable stretching, a close visual inspection may not detect the impending failure. Progressive fractures are often due to vibration of the vertical fin over a long period of time under overload conditions, such as those frequently experienced in combat.

I had drawn my tentative conclusions. We would need to send the remains of the tail assembly to the nearest metallurgical laboratory, which was located in Brisbane, Australia. There, laboratory examinations would either confirm or contradict my findings.

I was so intent on trying to resolve the technical mystery — the real purpose of this mission — that I was unaware of what was going on around me until I heard Elston call from the crest of the hill.

"Hey, Ed. Come quickly!"

Leaving the wreckage and running towards Elston, I noticed an expression of uneasiness on the faces of the police boys and carriers. Elston's face was extremely serious, as were Mills's and Timms's. McGovern, Brady, and Reed soon followed.

"What's up?" I asked.

"Scan that hill," Elston said, handing me the field glasses. "It'll make your bloody skin crawl."

Putting the glasses to my eyes, I saw what was causing the concern. My heart seemed to stop beating for a few seconds. Hundreds of black bodies scurried among the trees and bushes just one hundred yards away. The whole hill seemed to be moving.

"My God," I said. "Several villages must have banded together!"

"I'll bet they're not out hunting wild game," Timms said, taking out his handkerchief and wiping the sights on his rifle. "If they attack en masse we're as good as cooked."

I handed the glasses to McGovern. He started to raise them to his eyes, but stopped. "I don't need glasses. I can see them from here." He offered the glasses to Brady and Reed, who gestured that they didn't need them either.

"So what do we do now?" Brady asked nervously.

"I repeat," Timms cut in, "if they attack en masse we've had it." He paused. "Why don't you Americans collect as much of the dead airmen's remains as possible and bury them? Seems sort of a shame to let them lie out in the open, don't you think?"

I nodded to Timms in agreement. We four Americans raced back down the slope, stumbling, almost falling, over each other. Reed and McGovern, who had had the toughest time on the journey, no longer had any trouble keeping up with Brady and me.

The task of piecing together the crewmen's remains was gruesome. The airplane had hit the ground with such force that parts of the bodies were embedded into the ground. The odor was overpowering. When we were satisfied that we had identified twelve distinct bodies, we scrambled back up the hill to get carriers to help bury them. I explained to Elston that we needed at least ten natives to help us dig graves. He spoke to them briefly in Pidgin English, but they refused to go near the airplane. Elston fairly exploded, but they wouldn't reconsider.

"It's no use, Ed. They won't budge," Elston said. "And I don't think we'd better press the matter further. They'd rather walk back to Bena Bena without us than deal with those decayed bodies. I suggest you fellows bury them yourselves. Let's make the best of it."

That was that. I motioned to the other Americans. "Let's go. We don't have much time." We took small trench shovels from our packs and headed back down the hill, back down to the awful scene.

Digging in the hard ground was extremely difficult. But there wasn't much to bury. After scooping out twelve shallow graves, we wrapped the remains in GI blankets, placed them in the makeshift graves, and covered them with earth.

I suggested we each say a silent prayer for our dead comrades, but McGovern said one of the most beautiful prayers I have ever heard. There was nothing flowery about it; he lacked the well-practiced delivery of the preacher or priest. McGovern just stood there with his face toward heaven, his eyes closed, and talked to God.

"Heavenly Father, we ask that you take the souls of our fallen comrades into the bosom of your love, so that they may share eternal glory with you. Bless the families and friends these men have left behind and give them peace in their sorrow. Help us all to understand why tragedies like this happen and please, Father, let us never forget you are always with us, helping us overcome adversities, and giving us the strength necessary to do your will. Amen."

When McGovern finished, we set up pieces of loose metal and walk-around oxygen bottles to make headstones for the graves. Finally, we gave our dead comrades an appropriate military salute. Shots were fired to pay them a final tribute and farewell.

Our job finished, we climbed back up the hill. Elston was studying the steady advance of the headhunters and taking stock of our ammunition. I heard a bolt click as a shell was rammed into the chamber. Lock stood, grimly looking at his rifle. He patted the stock. "Betsy, if you ever shot straight, this is the time."

In spite of the grimness of our situation, I couldn't suppress a smile. No matter how the rest of us performed, I knew Lock could handle his share of the odds. I wasn't so sure about myself, since I was not as good a marksman as the Army would have liked. Still, the mass of natives was so thick that I was confident I could hit a few despite my less-than-perfect aim.

Brady, McGovern, and Reed took their guns from the carriers, inspected them, and filled their pockets with bullets from one of the packs. Timms and Mills stood quietly beside Elston as he studied the movements of the natives. Finally Elston turned back to us. "Gents, we have two vantage points to their one. I believe we might be able to stave off the attack. We've plenty of ammunition and guns."

"Don't you think you're being rather naive, Jack?" Timms said. "Even if we kill hundreds of them, some are bound to break through."

"If they've a mind to. But I have a feeling that if we mow a lot of them down they'll retreat and give up."

"That's a good feeling to have, but how do we know the hostiles will feel as we do?"

"We don't," Elston said. "It's a chance we'll have to take."

"No. We don't have to chance it," Timms said abruptly. "We don't have to chance it at all."

"Meaning what?" Elston asked.

"I'm going after a hostage."

"Like hell you are," Elston exploded. "You're staying here with the rest of us."

"I said I'm going after a hostage." Timms motioned to two police boys. They came over and he talked to them briefly in Pidgin English. Though obviously scared, they nodded, agreeing to go with him.

"Timms, you're not going. I'll shoot you first."

"Shoot if you like," Timms said, glaring at Elston. "But I'm going."

Then Timms motioned to the police boys, turned, and disappeared into the bush. Elston stiffened, made a move as if to raise his gun, hesitated, and gave up. "Damn fool," he muttered. "Crazy damn fool."

"What do we do now?" I asked. "Sit down and wait for them to return?"

"We'll wait. But we're also going to spread out and try to protect ourselves, Ed." Elston shouted some instructions to the carriers, who were huddled in a group. He motioned them toward the ravine where the wreckage lay. The natives didn't move, still not wanting to go near the scene of the crash. Elston jabbered in Pidgin English, waving his arms at them violently. Suddenly, almost in perfect unison, the carriers darted for the bushes. They had done what we had feared they might do in the face of danger, and now we were alone, except for the remaining eight police boys.

"All I wanted them to do was get down into the crevice for protection," Elston said wearily. "Instead, they chose the bush. We'll probably never know how many of them make it home safely."

With the carriers gone, it seemed deathly quiet. The eight police boys stood huddled, looking worried, and I wasn't feeling too confident myself. A sickening feeling had welled up in my stomach as I realized our only option might be to shoot our way out. I was thinking every bad thought possible about the Army, about pudgy Colonel Beam, safe and snug behind his polished desk, and about General Whitehead, who had sent us on this mission. If I get back, I thought, I'll give them a piece of my mind.

"Hey, Ed," Elston called from a few yards away. "You guys plaster yourselves on the ground and get ready. One group's closing in!" He yelled to the police boys to spread out and lie down with their rifles ready. It was so quiet we could have heard a twig break. From my prone position, I couldn't see anything. I was beginning to wonder whether Elston was right about the natives closing in on us when something thudded into the ground behind me. Turning my head, I saw a barbed arrow sticking up at an angle, at least half of the barbs imbedded in the ground. I was about to yell at Elston when a huge shower of arrows rained down upon us as though they had been fired from one great bow. Brady, who was lying near me, screamed and clutched his stomach.

I leaped up and ran over to him. He was moaning, "Oh, God! Oh, God!"

The shaft of a barbed arrow was sticking out of the lower part of his abdomen. I almost went limp as I bent over him. Then

I heard the Bren gun open up, and the crackle of rifle fire drowned out Brady's groaning. As I leaned closer I heard him gasp, "Help me, Major. Help me."

I suddenly felt sick. One glance at the wound convinced me there was nothing I could do for him at the moment. "Take it easy, boy," I said, trying to sound reassuring. "We have to take care of these natives or none of us will get out. Lie still. I'll be back in a moment."

Racing back to where Elston was blasting away with the Bren gun, I lay down beside him until there was a lull in the firing. The police boys were still slamming bullets into the rushing natives. I saw two of them fall headlong.

"Jack," I whispered hoarsely, "Brady's got an arrow in him. He's in bad shape."

"Anyone with an arrow in him is in bad shape," he answered blandly, running his gaze along the gunsight and letting loose another burst. "Forget about Brady and shoot."

In the excitement I had forgotten about shooting. I picked up my rifle, pointed at a dark figure, touched the trigger, and watched the native fall. Off to the left I heard crashing in the brush. Turning quickly, I ran my eye along the gunsight and was about to pull the trigger when Timms and the two policemen stumbled into sight, dragging a hostage behind them.

At that instant, all firing ceased. Elston leaped up, ripped his pistol from its holster, grabbed the native by his greasy hair, and slammed the pistol squarely into the man's face. The hostage began to bleed from a huge gash Elston had cut in his nose. Frenzied, Elston screamed at the native, "Sing out, you heathen! Sing out!" Again he struck the hostage with his revolver. The hostage defecated out of fear. "Sing out, you cannibal heathen!" Elston bludgeoned the man so viciously that I thought he might kill him before he could sing out and tell his people to throw down their weapons. I grabbed Elston's arm, trying to pull him away before he killed our ticket out of this place. Elston turned on me viciously.

"Leave me alone, Ed, or I'll kill you!"

I believed him, so I let go and stepped back. Elston struck the man's head again and held his hair tightly so that he would not collapse. Finally the hostage began to yell what sounded like a death chant in a high-pitched voice. Elston held the greasy head of hair tightly, the pistol held ready should the native stop singing out. After a few moments, unarmed natives began to give themselves up. Elston released the native, who fell limply into his own waste. More natives appeared without their weapons; from all appearances, the fighting was over.

Remembering Brady, I went over to where he lay. He was quiet. I bent over him and looked at his pained face. He was obviously feverish.

I sat down heavily on the ground, oblivious of Lock, McGovern, and Reed standing beside me. In a voice that seemed hollow and faraway I heard McGovern say, "My God, oh my God, I wish all these heathens would drop on the spot!" Reed took out his pocket knife and cut the arrow as close to Brady's body as he could. He threw the deadly shaft into the brush.

I stood up, glanced at Brady, and turned to the others. "If we can get him back to Bena Bena before the poison infects him, he's got a chance of recovering. We've got to try. If he doesn't make it, we'll bury him where the cannibals won't find him."

"I agree, Ed," McGovern assured me. "We'll build a litter and carry him ourselves. We're used to walking now. We can get him back."

Lock cut in. "I'm not worried about getting him back. I'm worried he won't last that long."

"I know what you mean, Lock," I said. "We'll travel faster. We'll travel at night."

"You're crazy," Lock growled. "We'll never make it."

"We've got to try. Even if it means walking without rests."

Mills joined us. "I'd like to put in my two cents' worth if I may, Major. Jack's telling these natives that unless they give us safe passage out of this place, we'll shoot every one of them. I think they'll go along with him, especially since we've already killed several natives. But I think we need to take two hostages in case any of them attempt to give us trouble on the return trip. The hostages can carry the litter."

"That's a good idea," I said. "But these natives aren't from the same tribe as the others we ran into."

"I doubt it'll make any difference. We have no other choice. If it works, we get home. If it doesn't . . ."

Mills went over and talked with Elston while we wrapped Brady in a GI blanket. Gil Timms took two police boys and went into the bush. A few minutes later they returned with two long, stout poles. Timms got another GI blanket, cut a few small wooden pegs, and punched them through the blanket to secure it to the poles. In just a few minutes, we had built a sturdy litter to carry Brady.

While Elston spoke in Pidgin English to the leaders of the group that had attacked us, the rest of us squatted on the ground. Lock picked up his rifle, casting a terrible glance at the native who appeared to be the headman. "I ought to make a third eye in his forehead," he said savagely, "the rotten . . ."

Placing my hand on his arm, I said, "It won't do any good. Jack's getting things under control. More killing won't help. Right now we have to concentrate on getting back as quickly as possible. Don't start anything, Lew. We may not be able to finish it. These natives aren't the only ones who attacked us. There are others out there, still armed." Lock laid the rifle on the ground, got up, and walked a few feet away to sit by himself.

Timms joined Elston and told him we should be on our way before something else happened. Elston nodded, pointed to two burly young natives, and said something to the chief in Pidgin English. The chief looked at Elston with his evil, glassy eyes and motioned for the two men to come forward. The chief's words sent the two hostages scurrying to the police boys, who formed a ring around them. Elston had bargained well. He dismissed the other natives and they slipped quietly into the brush and disappeared.

After placing Brady on the litter and showing the hostages how to pick it up and shoulder it, we gathered what rations we thought we would need, plenty of ammunition, and several canteens of water. The natives would return for the remainder of the packs. We shouldered our guns and began the walk back towards Bena Bena. We walked single file; five police boys went in front and the remaining five brought up the rear. With the police boys' constant vigil, there was little chance of the savages throwing down the litter and escaping. We had to make certain they did not escape. They were our only ticket home.

We elected to go back via a different route. Although we would still be in headhunter country for much of the distance, the route was more southern, closer to the coast. We hoped that the native telegraph would have spread the word. It did. Some of our carriers found us on the second day and resumed their duties. Elston didn't reprimand them for deserting us. There was no need of that. We were content simply to have them back with us. The natives helped us carry our physical burdens, but no one could relieve our mental burdens. We shouldered them alone. Most thoughts were of Brady, whose wounded body was being borne by the men who had wounded him.

We didn't have a single run-in with hostile natives on our return trip — for this we were extremely thankful. We only had to cope with the rough terrain, the dense brush, and the ever-present pestering flies. On the fourth day of the return trip, we came to the end of our journey.

In the late afternoon of the eighth day of our mission, we sighted Bena Bena. Had Brady been well, I'm certain we would have cheered at the sight of the airfield and the shacks surrounding it. But there was no celebration until we passed the airfield and finally stopped at the ANGAU building. Capt. John Hall immediately noticed the exhausted and sad looks on our faces. We were terribly tired, having slept only intermittently for one night on the return, but that was of little concern now. I, for one, simply wanted to get back to Port Moresby, the place I had once detested but now looked upon as home. After the ordeal in the bush I knew I could tolerate anything at Moresby, even the Japanese air raids.

Medical personnel at the ANGAU Unit treated Brady for his wound. He showed real hope for a recovery. The arrow would be surgically removed when we reached Port Moresby.

Elston released the two hostages and sent them scurrying into the bush without giving them so much as a *giri-giri* shell. Part of me had hoped he would shoot them in revenge for what they had done to Brady, but I knew it wouldn't help. I watched them go, wondering if there would come a time when their territory would be controlled and the headhunting and cannibalism would end. Who could tell?

Captain Hall informed us that a C-47 had been to Bena Bena the day before and was scheduled to return the next day. We only had to wait a few more hours. I went to bed thinking I would be bothered by horrible dreams, but the strain of the trek had caught up with me. There were no dreams. Only deep sleep.

XIII

DEBRIEFING

The next morning I was awakened by the sound of airplane engines. At first, I thought it might be the noise of Japanese planes coming to bomb us, but as the craft passed over us I detected the unique, unmistakable sound of a C-47. I slid out of my sleeping bag and yelled to the others at the same time. When I ran outside I saw the most beautiful thing I had ever seen, an American C-47, arriving to take me home.

In just a few minutes we had collected what was left of our gear. We followed the two porters carrying Brady as they hastened toward the airfield. After short good-byes to Elston and Mills, we boarded the airplane. As the senior officer on board and the unit's operations officer, the assignment of pilots was my responsibility. Capt. Charles Baer, the pilot of the aircraft, asked if I would fly the C-47 back to Port Moresby.

"With the greatest of pleasure," I said. "You don't know how badly I want to wrestle this airplane around."

"How was your trip, Major?" Baer asked.

"Successful and difficult," I said. "Brady was seriously injured. I hope we're getting him back to Moresby in time. How was the weather coming up, Baer?"

"Okay, but the buildups over the mountains were beginning to form. We may have some twisting and turning to do on the way back."

I went to the cockpit and got into the pilot's seat. I wanted to feel the grip of the wheel in my hands, to feel the power of the engines pulling me through the air. I wanted to release the anger I had bottled up over the last eight days.

When we landed at Port Moresby, the first person I saw was Colonel Beam.

He shook my hand vigorously. "How'd the trip go?" he asked enthusiastically. "Did you get what you went after?"

"And more," I said, wishing I were talking to anyone but Beam. "Lots more."

Lock, McGovern, and Reed sidled up to us. "Where's Brady?" Beam asked.

"In there," I answered, pointing to the C-47.

"Fine. I'd like all of you to brief me as soon as possible. Then the general wants to see you at his office. He's called twice already."

"We'll be there, except for Brady, that is. You see, he's been wounded — by an arrow. We're waiting for the ambulance."

"Wha . . ." Beam sputtered, his face turning red and his jaws beginning to twitch. The cigarette fell from his lips onto the ground. I ground out the fire with my shoe.

"An arrow in the belly," I continued. "It happened days ago, near the crash. We had a fight with the cannibals. Brady caught the arrow right at the beginning of the fight. He's in bad shape. He may not pull through."

"That's bad," Beam said. "The general is going to blow up at that news."

"I don't give a damn," I replied. "We did the best we could. We did everything in our power to prevent this from happening."

Beam's sour look and unsympathetic attitude irritated me. I was exhausted and worried — I didn't want to talk about it anymore. Beam's expression changed. His voice softened as he patted my shoulder.

"No one's arguing with you, Impo. Go ahead and sack in awhile. I'll fix things up with the general. If you say you can be ready to go to his headquarters at 1300, I'll see that someone wakes you and drives you there. I'll take care of Brady, too. It's the least I can do."

My irritation toward Colonel Beam subsided as quickly as it had arisen. Once again, I realized that Beam was a man who defied categorization. One moment he was a brusque, forceful, overly assertive man; the next, a compassionate, understanding friend. Walking away with the others, I wondered if I would ever understand him. I also wondered if the Army would ever see fit to replace him as group commander.

We slept through the lunch hour and, at 1245, an enlisted man woke us and said he had a vehicle to take us to command headquarters. In five minutes we were bouncing along the pitted dirt road.

When we walked into the aide-de-camp's office, the young captain looked at his watch and glared at me. "Major, you're five minutes late. You were supposed to be here at 1300. You've kept the general waiting."

"Kept the general waiting!" I walked up and stood toe-to-toe with the captain. There was nothing I wanted to do more than deliver a blow to his chin. "Captain, I think you and I had better have a little talk after the old man finishes with us. There are a few things about Army life — military courtesy and such — that you should know. One thing I'll tell you right now: I know I'm five minutes late; but since I'm a major I believe it would behoove you to let the general do the reprimanding. Later on I'll tell you about something that happened to us a few days ago while you were sitting here in your smug little office with nothing more to do than shuffle papers and run from an occasional air raid."

The captain's face was almost white when I finished yelling. I realized that I had gone too far. He, like me, was a victim of circumstances beyond his control.

"I'm sorry, Major," he said. "You're exactly right. Please, sir, the general will see you if you'll just go inside."

I thanked him, trying to be as friendly as possible, and motioned to the others to follow. I saluted General Whitehead and he directed us to sit down at the conference table.

"Gentlemen, I'm glad you're back." He paused. "I thought there were five of you."

I interrupted him. "General, you mean Colonel Beam didn't tell you about Brady?"

"Brady? No, he didn't. Where is he? I wanted all of you at this briefing."

"He's in the hospital having a poisoned arrow removed from his belly. He was wounded by a native in uncontrolled territory." I got up and went to the wall map and placed my finger on a tiny dot. "About here, General."

Whitehead looked at me as though he were looking at a ghost. His lips parted slightly and a look of utter amazement crossed his leathery face. "Brady . . . wounded by an arrow?"

I briefed him about the fight at the crash site and how we had managed to get away from the natives. The general listened intently, fumbling with his fingers, twisting them violently at times, exhibiting a tremendous amount of nervousness. When I had first walked into the room I had made up my mind to tell the general what I thought of his decision to send us into uncontrolled country. I no longer felt so belligerent, so angry.

I saw the taut, anxious expression the general wore. In the excitement and anticipation of the first briefing, the general had appeared lackadaisical about the war. Now I was doing the talking and the general was listening. I could observe his reactions as I related the gruesome story of Brady being wounded. When I finished, the general continued to stare at the map. He seemed to have forgotten that the rest of us were there. He looked worried and harassed; the burden of war seemed to weigh upon him. Finally, passing his hands wearily across his face, he asked, "Did you learn the cause of the accident?"

"Yes, sir. I think we found the cause." I explained that we had brought back parts of the wreckage to send to Brisbane for analysis. "We can't be certain, however, until we get the results."

The general looked at the wall map. "I hope we can determine the trouble. We've lost more than enough airplanes in those hills already." He paused for a moment, brushing a hand through his gray hair. "Now for the question about the bodies."

"We buried them, sir," I assured him, "and gave them a proper military funeral as best we could under the circumstances . . ."

"You must all feel pretty resentful toward me for having sent you on this mission."

"I'm afraid we did, General. In fact, you were quite the subject of conversation."

"The truth is, you hated my guts," he said, looking at me sternly.

"For awhile. There's no use lying about it. But we've had time to think."

"You mean since you got into this room a few minutes ago you've had time to think."

"I guess that's about it, sir."

"And how do you feel now?"

"Like I said, we've had time to think. You've got more problems on your mind than us, General."

"It wasn't an easy decision, sending you up there. You know that."

"I know," I said. This dedicated man was responsible for all air activities in New Guinea, and it was his good judgment that would ultimately win us the war.

Everyone in the room began to relax. Perhaps General Whitehead was more understanding, more concerned for our safety, than we had given him credit for. He slid his chair back from the table and lit a cigar.

"There's one more thing I'd like to know, gentlemen. Was there any evidence that the cannibals had eaten parts of the bodies?"

"There was evidence, yes, at one point during the trip, but

we never confirmed it. Our intention was to capture a native at the scene of the crash to learn more . . ."

"But you weren't able to because of the trouble?"

"That's right, sir."

"What is your honest opinion? Do you think they did?"

"We heard rumors that they had, but like I said, they were never confirmed. That's all. From what we saw at the crash site, I don't think there was enough left of the bodies to cannibalize."

"I could send a fighter squadron up there and teach those natives a lesson they'd never forget," he said.

"It wouldn't do any good, General. They wouldn't understand why we were doing it. Cannibalism is part of their way of life. Killing a few of them without explanation wouldn't change that."

"I agree with you, Imparato. Poor, ignorant, belligerent devils . . . it's funny, but I feel sorry for them in a way."

General Whitehead got up from his chair and pushed it against the table. "Gentlemen, I know you're not happy with me for sending you out there, but try to understand. I'm sorry for every man we lose here, but sometimes there is no way to prevent it. The bitter and the sweet go hand in hand here.

"I'm thankful that the rest of you got back unscathed. You accomplished what you set out to do. The success of the mission certainly justified the sometimes ruthless handling of the natives en route to the crash site and the small military encounter at the scene of the crash. I know it may sound like a small repayment for what you did, but I'm recommending each of you for the Legion of Merit. You deserve it.

"I can assure you that upon my recommendation you will each be presented with the medal and with a citation telling exactly why you were awarded it. I'll see that the Australians are decorated also. For myself, I thank you. That's about all I can say from an official standpoint. Unofficially, I can say that God was walking with you, or else none of you would have returned. Good day, gentlemen."

We saluted him and walked into the outer office. I went over to the aide-de-camp. "Captain, I don't think we need to have that talk after all." He got up and I stuck out my hand, trying to grin as best I could. "Keep the general in line, will you?"

"Sure, Major. I'll do that," the young captain said. "Come back sometime at coffee time. I'll buy you a cup."

When I got back to camp there was a message from the hospital. Brady had not survived surgery.

XIV
NEW CO

At 0800 I watched as the casket containing Brady's body was loaded on the C-47 shuttle to Australia. Colonel Beam and I stood near the cargo door, neither of us caring to talk. Four GIs moved the heavy box through the cabin door and lashed it down tightly. A few minutes later, several passengers boarded. They sat in the bucket seats opposite the casket, carefully leaving a berth for their fallen comrade.

"I made him a promise before we left for uncontrolled territory, Colonel," I said to Beam.

"A promise?"

"He was irked at being sent on the mission with us because he had to miss the shuttle. He had a girl down there in Brisbane, you know . . . he was deeply in love with her. I promised him that I would see to it he got on the next shuttle if he'd stop griping and go willingly."

"You're keeping your promise."

"Yeah, I'm keeping my promise. He's on the next shuttle, just like I said."

I took my handkerchief from my pocket and wiped away tears. I remembered having cried when I was a child over trivial things, and I remembered the embarrassment it had sometimes caused me, but I wasn't embarrassed to cry for Brady. I did, however, feel reassured when I saw Colonel Beam reach for his GI handkerchief and blow his nose loudly.

We watched the airplane climb high in the humid sky, turn

to the south, and fade away to a tiny speck in the distance.

"Impo, I'm very tired. How about you looking after things for the rest of the day while I sack in for a change? By the way," he added, "there's a set of orders on my desk making you a lieutenant colonel. Thought you'd like to know."

I had dreamed of the day I would be in the lieutenant colonel's bracket, but somehow, Beam's words about the promotion failed to excite me.

"Thanks, Colonel," I said unenthusiastically. "I'll pick them up later. Come on, I'll walk to your tent with you. I have to get something from my tent . . . some stationery and a pen. If you don't mind, I'd like to write Brady's parents."

"You have my permission, Impo. I'm sure you'll do a better job than I would since you were there when he was wounded."

We were in the middle of the compound when the siren began its mournful wail. The siren's pitch climbed higher and higher, piercing the early morning air until my ears felt as if they would burst. Men dashed from their tents and left the flight line heading for cover. I started to run, but slowed when I noticed Colonel Beam wasn't with me. I ran back to him and grabbed his arm. "Come on, Colonel! The Japs are close!"

"You go ahead, Impo. I'm too tired to run."

"I'm not going without you."

"Get going, Impo! That's an order. A direct order!"

I released his arm, ran to the nearest open foxhole, and jumped in. Two other officers were already there, crouched in the corner, waiting for the first explosions. I heard the whine of the Zeros as they streaked in for the kill. Peeping over the edge of the foxhole, I saw Beam sauntering casually toward us as he lit another cigarette. When he was within a few feet of the edge of the hole, he stopped suddenly and looked up at the oncoming planes.

"Beam! Get in this foxhole!" I yelled over the whine of the plane engines.

He didn't move.

"Colonel Beam! Get in here!"

"No damn Jap is going to chase me into a hole like a rat!"

"If you don't come in here I'm coming out after you!"

"I'm not afraid of them! Stay where you are, Imparato!"

I ducked just as the Japanese began to strafe us with machine guns. The bullets screamed over our heads and ripped into the tents. Others thudded into the ground. I balled up, lying as low as I could, trying to protect myself from the onslaught. My body trembled as though it would fall apart. I was as scared as I had ever been on the trip into uncontrolled territory. I had forgotten what it was like to sweat out an air raid in a foxhole, to listen to the whizzing of bullets and the crashing of bombs as they kicked showers of dirt over us.

The raid kept us pinned down for more than half an hour. The Zeros zigzagged across the airfield, preventing our airplanes from taking off to fight back. I could hear an antiaircraft machine gun chattering but I didn't hear a Japanese plane crash. They weren't using bombs on this raid, only machine guns, which meant that they were after us, not our planes. Hiding in the foxhole, I had no way of knowing how many men had been killed or injured. Each time the Japanese passed over us, screams of pain echoed across the compound.

When the raid was finally over, we crawled out of the foxhole to survey the damage. Colonel Beam lay sprawled grotesquely on the ground. A large pool of blood had formed beneath him. The machine guns had nearly cut him in two. Turning him over I saw the crushed cigarette still clenched tightly between his lips. His eyes were still open.

In an instant, the Japanese had unknowingly made me the new commanding officer. Picking Colonel Beam up in my arms, oblivious to the blood which poured down across my faded khaki shirt, I carried him to the hospital tent where the medics were working furiously. I laid the colonel down on an empty cot even though there was nothing the medics could do for him. I hoped they would wash the dirt from his face and attempt to restore to him the dignity of a commanding officer.

The next day, Sunday, was like any other day for soldiers in New Guinea. There was chapel service, work, and the predictable air raid. They never let up. Seven days a week, twenty-four hours a day, we could always count on Japanese air raids. At least something on this tour of duty was predictable.

Epilogue

Lab tests at the metallurgical laboratory in Brisbane, Australia, confirmed our initial findings from the expedition. The "chrommolly" forged bolts which held the rudders in place suffered a fatigue failure and severed. Our findings, and the lab's verification of them, resulted in the modification of the B-24 Liberator in the Pacific Theater of Operations.

Each of the Americans who took part in the mission was awarded the Legion of Merit.

Col. Roger Beam
Colonel Beam was killed in an air raid on Port Moresby, New Guinea, on May 18, 1943 — the day after we returned from completing our mission.

Maj. Gen. Ennis C. Whitehead
General Whitehead remained with the Fifth Air Force until the end of World War II and was later promoted to lieutenant general. He retired with that rank on July 31, 1954. General Whitehead died in 1964.

Capt. Lewis Lock
Captain Lock returned to flying duty after the journey and was back in the United States six months later. My attempts to locate Lock on my return to the United States failed.

Lt. Bill Brady
After writing Lieutenant Brady's family to inform them of the circumstances surrounding his death and receiving no reply, I made no further attempts to locate his family.

Lt. Paul Reed
Lieutenant Reed returned to the United States in February 1944.

Capt. John McGovern
Captain McGovern returned to the United States in mid-1945. He passed away in 1970.

Capt. Gil Timms
Captain Timms returned to the Wau gold mines after World War II and eventually retired to Australia.

Capt. Jack Elston
After our mission, Captain Elston returned to his position as commander of the outpost at Bena Bena. He remained with ANGAU, supervising the training and education of Papuans. He eventually returned to Australia.

Lee Mills
After serving as the unofficial cartographer of our journey, Mills continued surveying for the U.S. Army and ANGAU. He remained in New Guinea after World War II, and eventually received more sophisticated surveying equipment.

Many people have asked why it took me so long to write this story. My answer isn't a simple one. It's a combination of timing, scheduling, family, and career. During the long period of time between the events of this story and the publication of this book, the manuscript underwent numerous metamorphoses, which is a story of its own.

Our journey into headhunter territory began on May 9, 1943, at the direction of Gen. Ennis C. Whitehead, Commanding General of the Fifth U.S. Army Air Force. I first told the story of this mission in the form of a detailed diary I kept during the journey. The need for the diary was twofold: first, to serve as a basis for the official report I would have to write at the conclusion of the journey; and second, to record the events of this incredible mission for myself. In the back of my head, I was also thinking that if we were killed by hostile natives, the diary would serve as an explanation for our demise and a record of our efforts.

I used the diary to write the official report, which I submitted to General Whitehead after my return to Port Moresby, New Guinea. When I had completed my report, I asked each of the American officers who had accompanied me on the journey to write a report. I asked them to share their observations, their feelings, their conversations, and — in as much detail as they could recall — the significant incidents of the journey, especially those concerning our contact with the hostile tribes.

I combined the four reports I received from the American officers with my own and created a list of the events and conversations we all seemed to agree on. That list became the foundation of a detailed outline for my own future reference.

I did not write the book during the war because of the classified nature of our mission. I did not believe the story would pass military censors.

Upon my return to the United States in October 1945, I remained an active duty officer in the USAAF. With moves from base to base and numerous military schools to attend, there simply was no time for writing.

It was during my time in Panama as the Chief of Staff for the Caribbean Air Command that I finally found time to produce a manuscript. I wrote in the evenings after dinner, staying up as late as 2:00 or 3:00 a.m. My job entailed serving as the inspector general of all South American and Central American air forces, which meant a great deal of travel. I found time to write on the long flights to Brazil, Argentina, and Chile. I used the navigator's table to write for a few hours on each trip.

It was not until 1993, after my second bypass surgery and my doctor's admonition that I should live a quieter lifestyle, that I had time to concentrate on putting the manuscript into final form for submission to publishers.

The nature of creating a book — the lonely hours of writing, the research, the reliving of painful episodes — was hard, but it has resulted in the gratifying rebirth of a story of men and events in a remote corner of the world, a story that has remained with me for a lifetime.

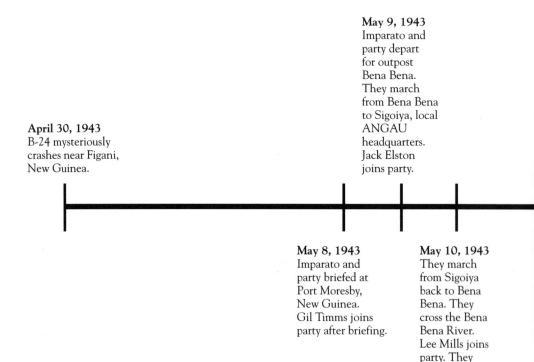

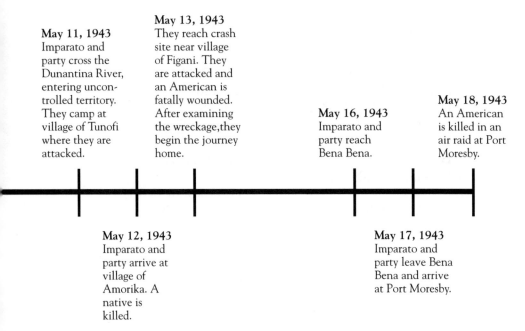

Index

A
Amorika, 102.

Australia and New Guinea Adminstrative Unit (ANGAU), 49, 51, 53, 70, 119-120, 133.

B
B-24 iii, iv-v, 109-111, 132.

Baer, Capt. Charles R., 121.

bari-bari shells, 42.

Beam, Lt. Col. Roger, 1-2, 3, 11-14, 15, 19, 23, 28, 29, 37-39, 42, 68, 74, 115, 122-123, 128-131, 132.

Bena Bena, 2, 8, 9, 45-46, 48-50, 56-57, 59, 76-77, 90, 108, 112, 119, 120, 133.

Bena Bena River, 63.

Bismarck Sea, iii.

Brady, Lt. Bill, 15, 35-38, 45, 53, 56, 66, 67, 70, 75-76, 80, 86-87, 94-95, 96, 98, 100, 101, 103, 104-107, 109-110, 113-114, 115-119, 121, 122, 124, 127, 128, 132.

Brisbane, 111.

Bulolo gold mines, 40.

Buna, vii-x.

C
C-47, 7, 42, 47, 48, 77, 120, 121, 122, 128.

Cocoanut Grove, x.

Coral Sea, Battle of, vi-vii.

cuma-cuma shells, 47, 57.

D
Dunantina River, 78, 80, 101.

Dutch East Indies, v.

E
Eichelberger, Gen. Robert, ix.

Elston, Capt. Jack, 49-50, 52, 53, 54, 55, 56, 57-59, 60, 61, 62, 78, 79, 81, 83, 84-85, 86, 87-88, 89-90, 91, 94, 95, 98-100, 101, 102, 105, 108, 111-112, 114-115, 118-119, 121, 133.

F
Fiji, v, vi.

Finschhafen, xi.

G
giri-giri shells, 57, 61, 62, 73, 120.

Glenn, Lt. Bill, 8, 10-11.

Guadalcanal, vii, x.

Guam, v.

gunda strips, 52.

H
Hall, Capt. John S., 51, 54, 119-120.

Horii, Gen. Tomitaro, viii.

Huon Gulf, vii, xi.

J
Jones, Lt. Carl, 8, 11.

K
kau-kau, 73, 107.

Kavieng, iii, xi.

Kokoda Track, vii, viii.

Korefego, 68.

kunai grass, 20, 52, 68, 71.

L
Lane, Lt. Thomas, 8-13, 22-24, 43.

Lock, Capt. Lewis, 14-15, 17, 34-35, 36-37, 53, 56, 66, 70, 75, 80, 86, 87, 94-95, 96, 98, 100, 113, 117, 118, 122, 132.

M
MacArthur, Gen. Douglas, iv.

Madang, 48, 50.

Marshall, Gen. George C., iv.

McGovern, Capt. John, 14, 37-38, 52, 56, 67-68, 71-72, 73, 75, 80, 101, 102, 109, 111-112, 113-114, 117, 122, 132.

McKinley, William, 77.

Message to Garcia, A, 77.

Midway, Battle of, vii, x.

Milne Bay, vii.

Mills, Lee, 61-63, 64-65, 67, 86, 100, 102, 103, 106, 111-112, 114, 117-118, 121, 133.

N
Nadzab, xi.

New Britain, iii.

New Caledonia v, vi.

New Ireland, iii.

"number one boy," 58, 61, 64, 79-80, 83-84.

"number one police boy," 56, 93.

"number two boy," 58, 79, 93, 96, 97-98, 99.

O
Owen Stanley Range, ii, vii.

P
P-38, 7, 11, 17.

P-39, 31.

P-40, 31.

Papua, ii, 104.

Papuans, 104, 105.

Pidgin English, 49, 53, 59, 71, 85, 86, 87, 89, 91, 94, 95, 101, 112, 114, 115, 118.

Port Moresby, ii, vi, vii, 1, 2, 11, 20, 68, 120, 133.

R
Rabaul, iii-iv, v, vi, xi.

Reed, Lt. Paul, 15, 37-38, 53, 56, 67, 72, 75, 80, 101, 102, 105, 109, 111-112, 113-114, 117, 122, 132.

Rowan, 77.

S
Saidor, xi.

Salamaua, vi, xi, 7, 42, 50.

Samoa, v.

Sigoiya, 51, 54, 56, 61.

Singapore, v.

sing-sing, 73, 90.

Solomon Islands, vii.

Solomon Sea, iii.

Spruance, Adm. Raymond A., vii

T
Timms, Capt. Gil, 40-41, 44-45, 47-48, 50-52, 56, 58, 60-61, 66, 68, 69-70, 72, 76, 77, 86, 87-88, 92-93, 98-101, 102, 103-106, 111-112, 114, 116, 118, 132.

Tokyo Rose, 32.

Tulagi, 84, 101.

Tunofi, 84-85, 87, 90, 101.

W
Wau, xi.

Wau gold mines, 40.

Whitehead, Brig. Gen. Ennis C., 7, 14, 15-19, 22, 41, 76, 115, 124-127, 132, 133.

Woodlark-Trobriand Island group, xi.

Z
Zeros, 7, 9-10, 11, 30, 31, 32, 33, 47, 50, 129-130.